For The Sins *of my* Mother

MARIE THERESE R

I would like to dedicate this book to the many girls that passed through the gates of Nazareth House and also my many friends, without whom this book would not have been made possible.

I thank you all from the bottom of my heart.

Published 2014 by Colourpoint Books
an imprint of Colourpoint Creative Ltd
Colourpoint House, Jubilee Business Park
21 Jubilee Road, Newtownards, BT23 4YH
Tel: 028 9182 6339
Fax: 028 9182 1900
E-mail: info@colourpoint.co.uk
Web: www.colourpoint.co.uk

First Edition
First Impression

A catalogue record for this book is available from the British Library.

Designed by April Sky Design, Newtownards
Tel: 028 9182 7195
Web: www.aprilsky.co.uk

Printed by W&G Baird Ltd, Antrim

ISBN 978-1-78073-065-3

Front cover main image:
Courtesy Daily Mirror. Picture by Justin Kernoghan.

CONTENTS

Foreword. 7

Preface. 13

1 Growing Up In The Orphanage 15

2 The Real World 71

3 An Innocent Released. 83

4 The Breakdown 97

5 The Struggle To Succeed. 112

6 The Torture Continues 135

7 Freedom At Last 141

8 The Meeting 161

9 Shattered Dreams 189

10 In Search Of Answers 200

11 The Final Journey 215

Epilogue 233

*Some names have been changed in this book
to protect the privacy of the individuals involved.*

FOREWORD

MARIE THERESE ROGERS-MOLONEY IS one remarkable woman. A life force. She is inspirational to all who know her. It is time her unique qualities – her empathy, her delight in just living, as well as her courageous ability to surmount one obstacle after another – were introduced to a wider public. You will adore her.

I first met Marie Therese in August 2010 and she told me her story then. It was compelling. I sat transfixed while Marie Therese ran through the key moments in her life. There were moments of dreadful sadness and pure unadulterated neglect that spoke of the secret and savage Ireland. This is the Ireland of 1950 that delivered an infant child to a Belfast baby home and then put up tall walls around her, and thousands of others, so we wouldn't be reminded of her existence.

A holy place. Indeed.

But don't think of this as a sad book. Even as she recounted the difficulties she endured as a child in the Nazareth orphanage she managed to maintain a lightness in her voice, a detached, almost humorous tone. I think that she had an ability to somehow distance herself mentally from the dramas that often threatened to overcome her. This, I believe, is what saved her from the fate of many others who went through the Irish orphanage system.

Leaving Belfast's Nazareth home at 17 ½ without an education, without money, without family, she was to find herself swept into a sort of half-life existence. Think of an innocent cast into purgatory. It seems fate was doing its very best to quash this young woman's spirit, to kill all hope. And yet somehow she managed to keep that necessary spark of self-belief and notion of self-worth alive long enough to make the most of the odd blast of kindness and empathy that would eventually transform her life.

Marie Therese is a fighter. So when as an adult she decides to go and finally get an education that had been denied her, you imagine that she will succeed. But who would have had her perseverance? When she failed her all-important English O Level exam it didn't matter. She had to take it again. And so she did. Time after time. All told she sat the exam 11 times before she finally passed. And then onwards with her.

No one else could have mustered that faith required to sit down and confront that exam paper so often, despite the almost predictable outcome. No one but Marie Therese. That speaks of the unbroken spirit, the continuing faith in her own qualities as a human being. She has that self-belief.

It is such a significant point, because not only does it give her such a wonderfully positive blast of energy personally, it also ensures, unlike many books of this genre, that despite the sometimes quite dark episodes, there is always in this work the hint of something brighter around the corner. When that hint of brightness finally explodes into glorious sunshine it will have you by the emotional collar.

For me the key episode in the book unfolds in Cloughjordan, Co Tipperary. It begins in a pub and continues through country roads to a small farmhouse. Ugly, cruel Ireland dies in the scenes that follow. You will eavesdrop on one of the most astonishingly personal but joyous moments you will ever encounter. It is charged with truth and love and happiness, all in stark contrast with the deceit and vanities of the other Ireland.

And yet there is no melodrama in the scene – or indeed any other. There is no sense of self-pity, just a powerful woman battling forward through life. Music has sustained her too. She plays the accordion, the guitar and the bodhran. And she sings too. So don't read this book if you expect a catalogue of misery. Marie Therese, after all she had been through, finds a way to see the positives no matter what is thrown at her.

I have met many other survivors of the four Nazareth homes in the North of Ireland. Few have coped as well as she has but they now at least have a forum to tell their stories: the Historical Abuse Inquiry (HAI). It is examining abuse in residential institutions here from 1922 to 1995. It began its work in 2014, Marie Therese intends to give her evidence in early 2015.

One key plank of evidence has already been given, by Sister Brenda McCall, representing the Sisters of

Nazareth congregation. She told the inquiry that some of the evidence of former residents from the homes in Derry had been "very shocking and harrowing for us".

When asked if there had been physical abuse by some nuns, Sister McCall replied "unfortunately, yes". When Sister McCall was asked if an apology for any physical and sexual abuse committed at Sisters of Nazareth homes should also address any claims of emotional abuse or neglect, the nun replied:

"Totally and absolutely. It's clear that at certain times and with certain nuns, things were just not right," she told the inquiry.

So we all agree, it's time for some flinty truth telling. Let the journey begin.

Darragh MacIntyre
November 2014
BBC Panorama

TO BE PREGNANT AND unmarried today is a fairly common occurrence and certainly nothing to be ashamed of. But to have a baby out of wedlock in rural Ireland during the 1940s and 50s was considered a grievous sin. So it was for Marie Therese's mother. She lived in a small village in the South of Ireland. Her husband had died a few years previously and when she discovered that she was expecting a baby she had no alternative but to hide herself away in an urban city where she would not be known. She gave birth to Marie Therese alone in Belfast in 1950, at the age of 39, having committed a grievous mortal sin. She had beaten the shame that would most certainly have befallen her in her little village community. Indeed her family knew nothing of the birth taking for granted that she was away on business at the time.

The infant was left in the care of nuns in an orphanage. What the mother's plans were for the baby will now never be known, but Marie Therese grew up to face a life of deprivation and hardship. She had clothes to wear and food to eat but she never had the comforting arms of a loving mother around her. Despite all the hardships she faced, for 37 years there was a strong spirit within her longing to be set free. She finally flung off the shackles that had bound her and enjoyed life to the full for some years. But that was all to change and she lost that hard-earned freedom. This time there were no high walls hemming her in, it was the pain of disability that prevented her from living a life she had just begun to taste and enjoy.

I began to know Marie Therese around the time when her illness became much worse. I have watched her increasing pain and disability curtail her lifestyle. The one thing that amazes me is her strength of spirit and determination that seems to have kept her going during those long years of difficulty. She will not be kept down and her achievements are testaments in themselves. Her story is a sad one, and it will bring tears to your eyes. And yet it is a joy to read, and to witness the way she overcomes every difficulty that presented itself. Marie Therese and her indomitable spirit is an example to us all.

Barbara Thompson
Social Worker

PREFACE

I COULD HARDLY SLEEP that particular night in the August of 1994, although I should have been well used to receiving exam results by now. Over many years I had repeated and failed the same exam, so if I passed I was going to make good use of it and if I failed, well I was just going to try again. Yet somehow something felt different this time and I was feeling surprisingly optimistic.

The post was late arriving that morning and while I waited patiently, I reflected back on the very first time that I sat this exam. I hadn't studied for anything since leaving the special school but in 1977 I sat my English exam. I obtained a Grade D but I knew in my heart that if I stuck at the studying it would eventually work to my advantage. If I could cope with the exam failure I would be able to cope with other obstacles in my life.

My thoughts were disturbed by the sound of something falling into the letterbox. As I held the letter in my hand my immediate thought was is it another fail? Another part of me dared to hope, after all this was the first time that I had studied English Language as a correspondence course. Could this be the turning point?

I opened the envelope and stood staring at the official writing on the piece of paper. The letter C seemed to have increased dramatically in size. Checking it several times I realised, yes! I've passed! After all the years of repeating I had finally achieved the grade I so wanted. I didn't know whether to cry, scream or laugh, and to think, at the time I studied for the exam I was suffering from chronic back pain. Was it because I had peace of mind and no Jean preventing me from achieving what I wanted to do for me? I'll say to anybody out there, where there's a will there's a way, and with hard work and determination your goal can be achieved.

Now, I was ready to settle down and concentrate on writing my own story, something I felt unable to do beforehand. By sharing my shattered dreams, hopefully they can finally be put to rest. When I started putting pen to paper I never for one moment thought it would take over eight long years to finish writing my story. Writing my autobiography has helped me therapeutically and also in some ways emotionally. The day I left that orphanage I swore to myself that some day I would discover who I really was and I was determined to find my true identity. Little did I realise that the search for answers would take almost 47 years.

In many respects, this story was written on behalf of the hundreds of girls who grew up with me in the orphanage and are still searching for answers. As I continued writing I was to discover much more about myself, and my roots, unaware there was a much bigger story to unfold! Let me take you along my journey of discovery.

Chapter One

GROWING UP IN
THE ORPHANAGE

My life started in February 1950, in a small private nursing home on Clifton Street, Belfast, called Lisieux. The name Therese was taken from the name Lisieux. A few days later I was carried in the arms of a complete stranger from the nursing home and placed in St Joseph's Orphanage for Infants on the Ravenhill Road. At the age of two, I was put into a pram with other infants and brought up the Ormeau Road to Nazareth House, the bigger orphanage for girls, where I was to spend the following 17 ½ years.

When I read and hear stories now about the Catholic priests appearing in court for the terrible acts they imposed upon the vulnerable children in their care, I thank God I wasn't one of them. However, the girls I grew up with and I were unfortunate in other ways, suffering physical and mental abuse with no way of defending ourselves.

This is how the regime worked in the orphanage: Girls stayed in the nursery from the age of two to five, before being transferred to the children's department. I can remember the nursery dormitory quite well, with cots along the window and down the middle of the room. I also recall being bathed in a large tub at four years old, about four at a time and sitting on a wooden table to be dried by a big girl. I found the move to the children's department quite traumatic and remember standing terrified that day in one of the schoolrooms before being directed to the juniors's dormitory. Once there, I was given my number, 51, which I had to remember for the rest of my time in the orphanage. Every time we washed ourselves we had to stand in front of a nun, turn our knickers inside out for inspection and shout "51 Sister".

The juniors were in one large group and the seniors in another group, and shortly after I arrived from the nursery, three large groups were formed. Each group was named after a Saint – Our Lady's, Saint Ann's and Sacred Heart's. There were about 30 children in each group, ranging from 5–16 years. Each group had one nun in charge of them, who slept in a small cell at the end of the dormitory. Once girls left school at 15 they were then sent to what was known as the girls's place. The only difference with their dormitory was that they had the privilege of having a curtain around their bed. Unfortunately, I didn't get to go to the girls's place. I didn't leave school until I was 16 and having attended a special school, I was treated differently, so had to stay in the children's department until I left the orphanage. The nuns didn't realise or perhaps care that, by not letting me move on into the girls's place, it would affect me later in life.

We all dressed the same, although in different colours. We wore a pinafore to protect our clothes but got into trouble if the pinafore was dirty and often had to keep our sleeves rolled up. The children did all the cleaning within the huge building and all we knew was scrubbing, waxing and polishing from the age of seven or eight years old. All the dormitories had to be cleaned once a month, along with classrooms, landings and the old toilets in the playground. Not just a lick, but scrubbed, waxed, polished and then inspected. I remember vividly a row of us kneeling down and going up and down the floor, singing or saying poems in rhythm to the movements of mops and polishers.

There was a weekend ritual: Saturdays were spent fine combing each other's hair, polishing shoes, darning socks and if it was the end of the month, changing all the beds. Friday evenings were even harder because the large stone corridor leading to the children's department had to be scrubbed and polished, which took hours to do. During this time Sister Luke, who was the senior nun, always stood watching to see that the work was carried out to her satisfaction and on many occasions, depending on her mood, she would make you scrub the hall again. She was the Principal of the school within the orphanage. She was of average height, with very high, red cheeks and a solemn expression. I never saw her smile during my time there.

One evening, while scrubbing the long corridor, the stick of my mop broke. Unfortunately, Sister Luke was right beside me and another girl called Ann, who was standing beside me. I glanced up at Sister Luke, terrified of what might happen. Her eyes were as cold as ice and her response was even colder, "I know where you will be next madam, Muckamore Abbey." That frightened me because I knew that Sister Luke was the one who could make things happen, had the power to do what she liked and there was nobody to question her. However, she didn't send me to Muckamore, which was a large institution for the mentally insane. A few of the girls had already been sent and two girls are still there today.

On another occasion I got into some mischief and was ordered to the notorious storeroom to await my punishment. Time passed and there was no sign of Sister Luke to carry out her punishment, so seeing lots of large boxes in the store, I climbed on top of them and sat there watching my friends playing in the playground from the window. More hours passed, the playground emptied and night was beginning to fall. After what seemed like an eternity I heard a key turn in the lock, I jumped up and to my relief I saw one of the older girls enter and not Sister Luke. "Get out," she said. Obviously Sister Luke had forgotten about me but being locked in that storeroom was punishment in itself. I even missed my tea that evening and was starving but could do nothing about it. At least I wasn't physically disciplined, which was a common form of punishment by the nuns.

One night in St Ann's dormitory, another girl called Anne, was told to shout out the decade of the Rosary. When she didn't comply with Sister Luke's order, Anne was told to go out to the bathroom and wait for her there. After some time Sister Luke appeared and told Anne to kneel down, which was quite common as you got punished. Anyway, Sister Luke canned Anne and when Anne didn't give in by crying, the beating got worse. Eventually Anne screamed at Sister Luke, "I hate you and I am running away from this awful place to find my mammy!" Sister Luke's response has left a dreadful psychological effect on Anne ever since. Turning to Anne, Sister Luke moved right into Anne's personal space and with a stern face retorted, "And where do you think you are going to run to madam? Sure nobody wants you and your mammy dumped you here."

Anne was a very quiet girl with black hair and pale skin. She was also very attractive and had lovely blue eyes; in fact she looked like an Irish Colleen. Anne left the orphanage before me and ended up working in the Civil Service. She married and had two children of her own.

Lily Ann was one of the older girls and one day she was sent for by Sister Luke. Lily Ann knew that it was only for one reason; a beating. She was being beaten by this nun when Sister Elizabeth entered the room and asked, "Do you need help?" Both nuns lashed out at the girl who didn't even know what she had done to receive such a thrashing.

From the age of seven I had terrible nightmares. They went on for many years and were always the same; I was behind something very dark and couldn't escape from this darkness. My cries woke me every time. However, it wasn't until many years later that my friend Mave supplied me with the answer to my nightmares. She told me that one day while playing in the hall, the Sister in charge clapped for us to stop playing. That was how things were done, when the nun clapped we immediately stopped what we were doing. Anyway, as we all stood quietly, a young couple entered the hall. They walked around looking from one child to the other before coming over to me. When they showed interest in me, the nun made me go with them but I screamed at the top of my voice and ran behind the nun to hide from these strange people. The darkness was the black habit the nuns wore. Their black habits covered their whole body, revealing little skin. We were only used to seeing them but not people from outside dressed in fancy clothes.

One day we were playing in the hall, which was only permitted when there was very heavy rain. We were making our own fun when the clap came. We all stood to attention and three girls were called to the front of the hall, told to get up on the stage and bend over. We had to stand and watch as a nun pulled their pants down individually and walloped their bare bottoms until she was exhausted. All we could see were very red and sore bottoms. I was terrified and wondered when it would be my turn!

Tuesdays and Fridays were bath days. There were three bathrooms, which had four large baths. The baths would be filled with water before an older girl or one of the nuns would pour Jeyes fluid into the water. You had to wear an old pinafore in the bath so that you didn't reveal any skin. While one girl sat at the edge of the bath washing her legs, two other girls held up a draw sheet and another girl sat down in the water. By the time the last girl of the whole group was bathed, the draw sheet was soaking. Your body was stinging with the effects of the Jeyes fluid and it left a dark brown mark around your waist. Once you were bathed you stood in front of the nun, turned your arms over and showed your ears, neck and your pants. They inspected you again and sent you on your way.

I was quite swarthy and one day Sister Elizabeth was in foul form. She grabbed me by the scruff of the neck, took me to the sink and starting scrubbing my neck until it nearly bled. On another occasion during the summer time, one of the older girls, Mary, was told to scrub my neck because Sister Elizabeth said it was dirty! Sister Elizabeth had come from the boys orphanage, which was on the Ravenhill Road. She wasn't too bad with us but the older girls had it very tough with her for many years. She was quite sarcastic at times and would often make a spectacle of you in front of the class. If you didn't pay attention in class the nuns would get you by the back of your arm and nip it so hard it brought tears to your eyes and left a terrible bruise.

The order of the day was Mass first thing, Benediction in the Chapel in the evening and the Rosary at your bedside in the dormitory. On entering the Chapel I was always frightened of the dreadful chanting sound coming from a small side Chapel, only for the nuns. The lighting was so dim in those days that from where we sat you could only see the outline of the dark figures sitting with heads bowed and had no view of their faces. For long enough when I entered a Chapel I expected to hear this awful chanting and see ghostly black figures. Every time we entered the Chapel we had to wear berets and God help you if you didn't have your beret on. We often had to enter from the huge fire escape and on a stormy day the berets were often blown off, causing girls already in the Chapel to giggle, much to the disgust of the nuns.

Each group had their own place to sit in the Chapel and the nun in charge of the group sat behind them. Our group always avoided sitting in front of Sister Elizabeth, because as soon as you showed signs of boredom, didn't say you prayers in Latin, whispered or perhaps even dozed, Sister Elizabeth would reach over and nip your neck, or just pull an individual hair, which was very sore. I was on the receiving end of her nips quite often.

Sister Luke was in charge of picking some of us for the choir. I was never picked for choir or anything else she had control of. The only thing I was suitable for was pumping the church organ and that was hard work. If you didn't pump the organ quickly it slowed down and with services sometimes lasting for well over an hour, you could be pumping for a long time.

Every year at Lent the nuns went on a religious retreat, which meant they were more times in the Chapel than with us children. However, while this was going on with them, we were all ushered into the large hall three or four times a day, where we had to sit in circular groups. Although we weren't involved in the actual retreat we might as well have been because we had to sit in complete silence for hours each day for about a week. We sat darning socks and saying the Rosary while Mary Anne walked about making sure we kept the vigil. The only form of escaping from the silence and complete boredom was to ask permission to go to the toilet. Once out of Mary Anne's sight you stayed out as long as possible. I hated that particular time of the year and I hated Mary Anne. It became a ritual and from a child's mind I could never understand the reason for Lent, and always associated it with the conventional sitting in circles, praying and daring socks, while the nuns prayed.

Mary Anne was an old woman and had grown up in the orphanage. She was a very hard and cold person and in all my years in the orphanage I never saw her laugh or smile. She was about four foot nothing, had this strange limp and shaggy grey hair. She wore a huge black boot that looked as though it was raised on a brick and looked so out of place. We nicknamed her 'Mary Anne, Big Boot'.

She worked in the sewing room and was responsible for teaching us how to sew and iron. If the school blouses weren't done to her satisfaction then God help you.

After Mass we had to make beds, sort out the juniors, eat breakfast and get ready for school. From the age of 5 until I was about 11 years old, meals were taken in complete silence and if you were late or had to leave the room you had to shout your number to the nun first. Breakfast consisted of porridge, bread and butter. Dinner was often stew, with more lumps of fat than meat, but you didn't leave much on the plate because even the plates had to be inspected and if you didn't eat your food you were either made to sit down until you did or the nun put more onto the plate. Supper consisted of coco, bread and jam and that was about 5.30 pm.

One day one of the girls called Julie decided that she would ask for more bread. We didn't usually ask for much but Julie did and when Sister Elizabeth heard this request, she went mad. She walked over to Julie, went right into her personal space and shouted, "You want more bread?!" She disappeared and returned with the largest loaf of bread any of us had ever seen. With wide eyes we watched as she stamped over to Julie and slammed the loaf of bread on the table, nearly knocking the table over with her force. Just as Julie looked down at the loaf, probably thinking she had hit luck, the loaf was immediately swiped from under her eyes much to the laughter of the whole dinning room.

Julie seemed to have this thing about food. She discovered where most of the food was stored once it came into the orphanage and along with another girl sneaked into the store to see for herself. She couldn't believe her eyes when she saw the food – things like apples, oranges and lemonade – that the old men, women and nuns got, but not us. Julie had lovely curly dark hair and very red cheeks. When she left school Julie was sent to work in the sewing room and apparently later opened her own clothing company in Dublin.

The juniors went to bed between 6.30 pm and 7.00 pm and the seniors had to be in bed for 9.00 pm. As we had to pass the television room to get to the dormitories we weren't allowed to come out again, even if you wanted to go to the bathroom, because the older girls shouted at you to get back into the dormitory. We were as much frightened of the older girls as we were of the nuns. I suppose when the nuns took out their frustration on them, then they could only take it out on us.

I had a habit of rocking myself to sleep and always wet the bed. Every morning the girls who wet their beds had to rinse their sheets out in cold water in the bath and take them down to the laundry. There was a very tall, thin old woman called Millie who looked after the laundry. She had really long hair that had aged with her years and always wore it the same way, with a long twisted plait running down her back and a small black bow tied at the end of it. You could never sneak into the laundry, place your wet sheet into the tub and run out again because Millie sat just inside the door in a large rocking chair, with a cat on her lap and a huge stick resting against the chair, ready for use. I have to say in the whole time I went into the laundry Millie never used the stick on me but I was frightened of her. She had this massive lump in front of her throat, which was in full view for all to see. I think she never hit me because I never once made eye contact with her in all the years that I was there. As a child I felt she perhaps hated her own appearance.

I wasn't the only one frightened of Millie. Rosie, Molly and Lilly who worked in the laundry were so terrified of her that when she sneezed, all the machines were turned off, the workers stood and said, "God bless you Millie, may the devil miss Millie, may he never know you are dead till you're half an hour in Heaven." Millie would listen contentedly before saying, "Thank you girls, now back to work with you." Until I left the place my morning ritual involved hearing Millie say, "Put the sheets in the tub". The bed-wetting continued until I was 18 years of age, which added to the stigma I already felt.

At one point the nuns placed a large, strange cover on my bed containing small, fine wires. During the night if water hit these wires, a piercing alarm would sound. I hated it because it not only woke me but the rest of the girls in the dormitory and I was shouted at for waking them. This contraption certainly didn't help me. After a few nights of this anguish, I turned the machine off.

When I had the accident I would get out of bed, find a dry part of the sheet, roll my nightdress up, get back into bed and fall asleep. Obviously the machine didn't work and it was eventually taken off me and used for Julie. I also suffered terrible earache and headaches from a young age. Somehow it was made worse during the night and when it happened I would cry under the bedclothes because I knew there was nobody to turn to for comfort and help. You just suffered, because nobody heard your cries.

At the end of each dormitory there was a small cell, where the nun in charge of that particular group would sleep. I used to think that the nuns were bald because of the way they wore their religious habits. Never once did I see a tuft of hair, even their eyebrows until one night while Sister Elizabeth was in her cell and we were talking loudly to her annoyance, she banged the small window, telling us to keep quiet. Just before she banged the window, she peaked through the curtain and that was the first time I saw her without her habit on. Her head looked as though it was shaved and she looked awful.

There is one particular night that I will never forget. In the middle of the night, Sister Elizabeth called from her cell and told me to get up and dressed then wait for her in the bathroom. I was quite groggy and sleepy but did as I was told. I waited in the bathroom and after some time Sister Elizabeth appeared but she wasn't alone. Behind her were three little girls, the oldest not much younger than me, and the youngest looked about 4 years old. I knew instinctively that they were new girls because they looked so dirty and dishevelled. My heart bled for them the moment I saw them but it was as much a frightening experience for me as it was for the poor girls.

The nun stripped all three and I was told to fill the bath and add the Jeyes fluid. She and I bathed the three girls. The sight of the three sisters has remained with me to this day. The youngest of the three had terrible sores on her feet and all of them looked so frightened and bewildered. After they were bathed I had to get the two oldest up to the dormitory and into bed, while Sister Elizabeth took the youngest, screaming to the nursery. There was nothing I could do to ease the situation or even comfort the girls but I certainly felt sorry for them. It took some time before the girls actually settled but eventually they did and before long they were one of us. I heard later that their parents had problems and had left the children alone for some time before they were discovered. I must have been about 14 years old at the time.

Sister Elizabeth had her kind moments but unfortunately they didn't happen often. You never knew she was about the place until she was standing right behind you. One year at Halloween, the nuns were having a fireworks display for the older girls and the elderly people in what was known as the back yard. We were sent to bed at the usual early time of 6.30 pm, but some of the girls in our dormitory decided to sneak down the fire escape to watch the display from behind a wall.

After enjoying the spectacle, the girls headed back to the dormitory via the fire escape, only to be met half way by a very irate Sister Elizabeth. Despite only a few of them venturing out, the whole group suffered for it. We were wakened by her and made to kneel on the sitting room floor with our hands on our heads for the remainder of the night. She sat in a chair watching us and if anyone moved she bawled at you to stay kneeling and keep your hands above your head. It was worse than getting a good thrashing. We learnt the following day that girls from the other dormitories had to sleep the rest of the night on the fire escape steps, which were just outside the dormitory. I don't know which of the two punishments were the hardest!

Nighttime punishments were fairly common. I remember one girl called Clare being punished by Sister Elizabeth for not replying to a letter. Clare was quite a tall girl, with dark hair and dark eyes, and a was a few years older than me. She was very giddy and often in trouble for one reason or another. Like me, she had been in the orphanage from birth but her mother used to visit her quite often. I wondered but never asked why some children had visitors and many of us didn't. One time Clare's mother stopped visiting her and it was later learnt that she was ill in hospital. Clare received a letter from her mother and was told to write back to her but she didn't. When Sister Elizabeth discovered she hadn't replied, she was made to kneel in the aisle of the dormitory one night until she wrote the letter. This was while the rest of us slept. As darkness drew Clare climbed into bed, thinking Sister had forgotten about her, and fell asleep. After some time Clare was pulled out of her bed by Sister Elizabeth and made to kneel in the middle aisle for the rest of the night.

Weeks later Clare fell ill and was taken into hospital but not because of the punishment meted out to her. About a month after that we were wakened from our sleep in the dead of night and told to kneel at our bedsides. I thought we were in trouble but it was to pray for Clare. We said so many Rosaries because Clare had taken a turn for the worse. In fact, Clare had developed a brain tumour. We didn't understand the significance of her condition and were cross with her for having our sleep disturbed to pray. We used to envy others who ended up hospitalised, because on their return to the orphanage, the older girls used to spoil them. Clare thankfully recovered but was unfortunately left disabled, with her mobility and sight affected. I discovered that she later married and had two children. On talking to her, she remembered the many times that she complained of headaches and actually walked into the wall on several occasions, but nobody listened to her. In fact, she was scolded for 'acting silly', as they put it.

Lots of things seemed to happen at nighttime. Some of the things the girls got up to were very funny, like getting out to a dance on a Friday night, when everybody had gone to bed. They did this by sliding down a drainpipe that ran alongside the window of the bathroom used only by the older girls. A girl who didn't venture out with them saw that the window was always left unlocked for the dancers returning in the wee hours of the morning.

Margaret was one such girl who was determined to get to her dance. Margaret and her sister Lucy came into the orphanage when they were about eight and nine. I remember them arriving in the playground one day wearing different clothes from us. However, like all the new girls before them, it wasn't long before they were dressed just like the rest of us. As they had experience of the outside world, they didn't care what nuns thought about them. I suppose they had a good feel of the outside world by that age and had developed their own characters and personalities. In some ways this made them different from us because they hadn't conformed to the regime of the orphanage. Margaret in particular went against anything and anybody that was part of the establishment. She had brown hair, was thin and had a very defiant expression, while Lucy was smaller, with much lighter hair and clung on to her older sister for some time before making her own friends within the orphanage. Margaret certainly wasn't afraid to speak out and got into more trouble than enough because of it. She and Lucy were put into Sister Maura's group.

Like the rest of us, Margaret went to the local secondary school but after a few years she gained a scholarship to a convent grammar school in

Ballynahinch. None of us had sat any exams, even the 11 plus and to this day Margaret doesn't know how she and another girl Jenny got the scholarship. They were the only two sent to the school and they hated it. They had to stand outside the orphanage each morning for the bus to take them to Ballynahinch, which returned quite late in the evenings. After just a few weeks at the school both girls played truant and it wasn't long before the nuns were informed.

Margaret got the brunt of it and received such a hiding from Sister Luke that she retaliated and ran as fast as she could out of the orphanage to her uncle's house. He and his wife took Margaret to the local police station and guess what? A black taxi arrived with two nuns in it and took Margaret back to the environment in which she had been severely beaten. Unknown to the rest of us at the time, there was a holy war about the episode. Jenny wasn't beaten because her parents still kept in touch with her. Jenny and her sister had also come into the orphanage later in life. After this both girls were sent back to the local secondary school. Strange, but when new girls arrived we never thought to ask where they came from and why they were sent in.

As Margaret was the oldest she left the orphanage before Lucy, but once she was of the age of consent, she came and took her sister out of the place. Even that was an ordeal for Margaret, as Sister Luke made things as difficult as possible for them both. Margaret eventually married and became a district nurse and Lucy went to live in Scotland, married and had two children.

Anyway, back to the weekend escapes. The weekend outings continued until their little plan was discovered. Mary Anne slept in the same dormitory as the older girls and it was she who discovered what was going on each Friday night. She was always snooping about the place like a little spy for the nuns. She told Sister Claire, whose cell was in the older girls' dormitory. A nun was still supervising the girls who had left school and working about the orphanage. They were either sent to the kitchens, the laundry, the parlour, the old people's department or the nursery. Sister Claire ordered Paddy, the handyman to put a permanent lock on the window but that didn't deter Margaret and the other girls. It wasn't long before another means of escape was organised.

Mary Anne was like a nun but without wearing the habit. Her appearance frightened most of us, as did her manner. I am sure prisoners today have more freedom than we had as children. Mary Anne wouldn't have thought twice about clipping you across the ear when you were least expecting it and I was certainly at the receiving end of her hand on many occasions. Mary Anne hated it when you looked straight at her. She seemed to have the idea that you were staring at her and without warning she would give you a clout across the face, asking, "What you looking at?"

Every Sunday, weather permitting, we went for long walks up the Ormeau Road, down the road and through the Ormeau Park. We stopped there for an hour or so before getting into twos and heading up the Ravenhill Road to the orphanage. Before heading off we were always told never to talk to any 'outsiders'. We wore either red or grey coloured coats, which looked so old fashioned; talk about looking conspicuous. While walking we had to hold hands and hated the stares of the 'ordinary people'. Getting out of the place was great but even our time in the park was uncomfortable for us, as you would often hear parents saying to their children, "If you are bold you will be in the home with the bad girls and boys." There was an old graveyard half way up the Ormeau Road. I hated passing it because if we talked some of the older girls would threaten to push you in with the dead people.

One Sunday when I was about nine years old, we were coming up the Ravenhill Road when I desperately needed to go to the toilet. As you weren't allowed to stop, I had an accident. When we got back to the orphanage I was bathed in cold water; told to wash my clothes and get them down to the laundry. The same happened to my friend Carol on another occasion. We both remember this vividly. Going down to the laundry and facing Millie was terrifying to say the least, "Put the clothing in the tub and away with you." We were out of that laundry as quick as a flash! It was embarrassing enough having an accident, but to be punished for it was even worse.

Our primary school was within the orphanage and from the age of five I was placed into Sister Elizabeth's class, the class was for slow learners. There were about 30 in the class and most of the time was spent drawing, knitting, sewing and listening to the wireless. Sister Elizabeth would often lose her temper with us and out would come the stick. Her other punishment was to take both your wrists and, with force, make you hit yourself with your hands. After, she would say, "Now you hit yourself!" One day, she asked us to write a little story on anything. I wrote about my imaginary family, which consisted of a big brother and that was all. What did I know about a family? Years later Sister Elizabeth told me about the story and how I had ended it by saying, "This is the family I would love, but will never have." According to her she gave me top marks for it and it was shown to some of the other nuns.

At the age of 11 we were sent down the road to the local secondary school that had opened a few years earlier. Before it opened all the education was done within the orphanage, which meant that girls a few years older than me had all their education within the establishment. At least we had the opportunity of seeing beyond the orphanage walls. Our uniform consisted of homemade blouses, long skirts and Wellington boots, which we hated with a vengeance. The collars of the blouses crossed over and we had to wear large grey knickers with no leg elastic. We looked and felt so conspicuous, and the 'outsiders', as we called them, knew immediately we were the orphans from up the road. After some time we discovered a way of not wearing the Wellington boots. Every morning Sister Luke watched us get ready for school, she inspected our uniform and off we headed down the road to school. However, half way down the Ravenhill Road, there was a long lane, with hedges down either side, out of view from the public. This was an ideal spot to hide our boots.

After school, we retrieved our boots and went back to the orphanage, where Sister Luke waited each day. Our little plan went on unnoticed for quite some time until one evening we headed for the hedge after school to retrieve our Wellingtons only to discover them missing. We certainly weren't in any hurry to get home but when we finally did Sister Luke was waiting, and standing beside her was a row of Wellington boots.

As usual the punishment was scrubbing the landings and stairs of the children's department and others were sent to the storeroom for physical punishment. She would inspect the work and on one occasion I was told to scrub the stairs three times, after which I was exhausted. We never found out how she discovered our secret hiding place but we knew it wasn't the lady who lived at the end of the lane. Another hiding place was found which was never detected.

I remember on another occasion I was ordered to scrub all four landings and stairs and report to Sister Luke when the job was complete. She stood at the bottom of the stairs, looked at me and said, "Do you call that clean?" "Yes sister," I replied quickly. "Do them again", she said and walked off leaving me standing there. The power of this nun had was so incredible that it was the frightening.

At the beginning of one summer a group of us were called by Sister Luke and told to go down to the laundry. We had to stand over large wooden planks and wash all the jumpers by hand, which took hours, while the other girls were out playing. By the time we were finished there was no time for play because other work had to be done about the place. I think that there was a two-tier system, with children who had absolutely nobody coming off the worse than those with parents who kept in touch.

Something happened one evening in the playground, which has been imbedded in my mind ever since. A girl called Louise was summoned to the classroom that was also used as an office. When Sister Luke sent for any of the girls it was never a good thing so we all knew that Louise was in trouble. Sister Luke was always picking on Louise for one reason or another. After Louise went to the classroom a few of us decided to follow her. As we sneaked through the classrooms that lead to the one that Sister Luke was in, we could hear this terrible screaming. At one point we peeped through the frosted window and what we saw was so alarming that it could never be erased from a child's mind. Sister Luke had Louise by the hair and was cutting at it like somebody who had completely lost it, while Louise screamed. Once we saw what was happening we didn't stay two minutes for fear of being caught and having the same thing done to us.

Some time later Louise came out to the playground and all eyes turned to her. Her hair was in a complete mess and the expression on her face said it all. She took so much pride in her appearance and was always washing and working at her hair. She was quite tall and thin, with a long nose and beautiful dark curly hair that was her pride and joy. Sister Luke took this away from Louise and it must have hurt and humiliated her immensely. What I saw that day has remained with me for the rest of my life, especially the shock on Louise's face. I am sure Louise never forgot that episode either.

Despite the many sad moments, however, there were many funny occasions and we got up to plenty of mischief. There was a furnace under the building and some Saturdays we used to sneak down to have a smoke of paper. Imagine smoking paper! We could have easily set the place on fire but all we cared about was our wee smoke.

There was a huge yard leading from the laundry to the children's accommodation, which was enclosed with barbed wire. Beyond the yard there was a boys' club and every Saturday during the summer, after we had fine combed our hair, cleaned our shoes and darned any socks that needed done, we had to set up three large tubs of water filled with Jeyes fluid. Keeping only our pinafores on, we lined up in our groups to have our hair washed by the older girls. The boys used to hang out from the club windows, whistling down at us, much to the annoyance of the nuns in charge. We enjoyed the boys' company, even though we were embarrassed at them seeing us having our hair washed and dressed in pinafores. The nun in charge was exhausted shouting at them but the whistles continued to our delight! It was great fun knowing the boys could get away with misbehaving without being punished. Every Friday we could hear the music coming from the boys' club and the older girls used to shout from the dormitories at the boys entering and leaving the club.

Rosie was an older woman who worked in the laundry, which was at the back yard. She had grey hair, a slight limp and a floppy hand. Like us she had gone through the system from childhood and was now spending the rest of her life there. From a little girl I can always remember Rosie about the place. She probably wasn't that old, but as children she appeared much older to us. Every morning she set off to the laundry at the same time and on a few occasions some of us gathered at the dormitory windows overlooking the yard that lead to the laundry and sang at the top of our voices, "Pretty woman, walking down the street", much to the annoyance of poor Rosie. We had great fun watching her reaction. Turning in the yard she would shout at the seemingly empty windows, "If I get the hold of you, you'll be sorry!" She didn't know whom she was shouting at as we slid down below the windowsills giggling. I dread to think what would have happened if she got the hold of any of us. I learnt some years later that Rosie sadly died in the orphanage.

The Holy Rosary Chapel was right next to the orphanage. We used to climb on top of the climbers in the playground to watch wedding parties arrive at the Chapel, which was very exciting. There was a huge orchard at the rear of the Chapel and every year there were plenty of apples and pears for the taking. The orchard was out of view from the main part of the orphanage, so each year we took advantage of the rich pickings. A few of us would climb over the wall, while others kept watch for any of the nuns. Once over the wall and into the orchard, apples and pears were collected in their dozens and thrown over the wall for us to gather and share among our friends.

One day we relaxed our guard and the pears and apples were coming in their dozens when suddenly one of the girls shouted, "Quick, Lizzie's coming." She just seemed to appear from nowhere, and we dispersed in all directions. Meanwhile the girls throwing the apples over the wall proceeded to climb back, only to come face to face with Sister Elizabeth. One girl, Pat, in particular had so many apples that some were up her knickers. As Pat walked away to begin her punishment, the apples started falling to the ground. We could see this scene from the safety of the dormitory windows and I am sure Sister Elizabeth heard the laughs of us that day! As usual the punishment was scrubbing floor, polishing the pews in the Chapel or a good thrashing but needless to say, it didn't prevent us going for the apples and pears the following year.

Pat was a black girl and she had beautiful tight curly black hair and huge brown eyes. She was very tall and thin, and quite awkward in things she did. She was the type of person who would fall over her own feet. She always had problems with her ears and often attended the hospital. We used to feel so sorry for her because every time that there were important dignitaries visiting Pat was always put in the front line because of the colour of her skin and also because she looked so pretty and appealing to visitors. She hated being in the front line and also hated the fact that she was the only black girl in the orphanage.

One time Mave went into the bathroom and there was Pat scrubbing her skin and pulling at her wiry black hair. "What are you doing Pat?" Mave asked. "I hate being black and I hate this hair," Pat answered angrily. Still pulling at her hair she shouted, "I don't like the worms either." As far as we were concerned she was just one of us and the colour of her skin didn't matter.

Everything we did in the orphanage was supervised at all times and watching the television was no exception. Most of the programmes we saw were musicals, Cowboys and Indians, and Blue Peter. On many occasions while watching the television, Sister Claire, who called us 'girly', had a terrible habit of spoiling the storyline. If the good man shot the bad man dead, Sister Claire would respond with, "Oh sure he will be alive for his breakfast in the morning." We saw little television and the little we did see was often ruined by her comments.

Every so often a large screen was put up in one of the classrooms and we would watch a film, which caused great excitement. *The Lone Ranger, Easter Bonnet* and *Annie Get Your Guns* were great favourites. Yes we did enjoy the films, no wonder we played so much pretend Cowboys and Indians in the playground! And we were always singing. Another film I remember was the *Nun's Story*, which we saw over and over again. However, there wasn't much point in watching it because every time something was shown that we shouldn't see, Sister Elizabeth would cover the projector. She seemed to be the organiser of the large screen.

Christmas caused great excitement in the orphanage. In the classroom we had to make the decorations that were put up about the place. Well-known companies around Belfast offered to take children out for parties. Buses were organised to collect the children to bring them to and from the party. This meant you would be away from the orphanage for most of the day and that was a real treat. However, it was Sister Luke who decided who was going out to the parties and as I wasn't one of her favourites my name was seldom on the list. I used to avoid her as much as possible.

While the other children were at the festivities I, along with the few who didn't go, got the dirty jobs to do about the place. The lucky ones were sent to the sewing room to be fitted with a dress and told what time to be ready for the bus. There was a large mirror in the hall and one day, when Sister Luke was calling the names out, Louise was talking and Sister Luke shouted at her. Louise was standing behind the Sister and without thinking she stuck her tongue out. Sister Luke saw her in the mirror. Poor Louise didn't get out to many parties after that.

The companies involved in this yearly event included: Mackies Engineering Firm, Queens University in Belfast, the Ormeau Bakery and Nutts Corner, which was an old air base. Watching your friends going without you was terrible, although everybody went to the Mackies party. Going to the parties was the only time that some of the girls who had brothers in the boys' orphanage got the chance of meeting with them again.

Another party we all went to was the Black Taxis in Belfast. They organised a huge beach party during the summer time. Off we would set in a huge convoy of taxis, perhaps six or eight children to a taxi singing our hearts out until we arrived at Tyrella beach, where we stayed for most of the day and had such fun. Thankfully, nobody was excluded from the taxi party. Getting out to the parties was also respite from work. I wonder if any of those taxi drivers are alive today and would remember those years. I have fond memories of them and am very thankful for their generosity. By the time you got back from the parties it was straight to bed. We always got fruit and toys but once back at the orphanage the toys were collected and I don't remember playing with them. Unfortunately, after a few years, the parties stopped.

We preformed a concert every Christmas for the nuns, priests and other important religious guests. A man came from outside and those of us who were picked to perform were taught songs and our little individual pieces. One year to my amazement Sister Luke actually allowed me a very small part in the concert. To this day I can remember the short piece I had to sing. I was dressed in a parson's costume with a huge top hat on and from the back of the row had to dance to the front of the stage. I took the top hat off and twiddling my thumbs sang:

"Parson Ben Says Brethren,
I'll now send round the plate,
As this collection is for me,
The money I shall take!"

With a cheeky grin I danced around the other performers, collecting my money. The people in the hall were in uproar with laughter at this short verse and the fact that I was dressed as a man of the cloth made it more amusing to the audience. I didn't understand what I was doing but wanted to cry because they were all laughing at me. Yet at the same time I was pleased with myself for performing so well and not forgetting my simple lines. I must have been about 12 years old at the time. Learning these few lines was more important than learning my prayers at Mass, because we all prayed together in the Chapel but now I was singing alone and couldn't rely on the other girls to sing for me. It was a great feeling being noticed by so many important guests.

Even at Christmas we still got up to mischief on important occasions. Large boxes of costumes were stored in Sister Maura's classroom and we were told not to go near them. Curiosity always got the better of us and in we would go and have a good rummage through the boxes, taking the most colourful and best costume. Before long there were fights to see who got the best.

One day we were in the middle of squabbling over the costumes, when someone shouted, "Maura's coming!" The ones who couldn't get out the door quick enough dived into the boxes. Sister Maura grabbed us out and gave us such a hiding. She had a particular way of beating you and a bamboo stick was her favourite. After the beatings the stick left terrible marks on the skin. She would tell you to turn your arm over until it showed the tender spot before reining the cane down and God it wasn't half painful.

When Sister Maura punished you, she did her best to break you mentally. The beatings went on until you broke and when you didn't cry she continued until you did. One night in the dormitory Christine was talking and Sister Maura got the hold of her, dragged her to the front of the room and beat her continuously. Christine came into the orphanage as a five year old and developed her own wee character. Mave was in the same dormitory as her and wanted to cry out as Sister Maura beat Christine so hard but like the rest of the group could do nothing to help her friend. On another occasion, the girls counted to 100 before Sister Maura stopped beating a girl called Anne.

Another girl, Bridie McMullan, was always in line for Sister Maura's punishments but somehow it didn't seem to fizz her. She was in Sister Maura's group and the nun used to say to her, "Old Nick is inside you." It took a while before we all realised that Old Nick was actually the devil. Like me, Bridie was in the orphanage since birth and we were the same age. She was a real tomboy and always up to mischief. She had very short, dark hair and boyish looks, and was always trying all the nuns' patience.

We had a dog one time, which we called Nicky. Bridie absolutely loved the dog and took charge of it but he was never allowed into the place. One day he did get into the hall and had an accident. Sister Maura decided that she would show us how she could punish the dog. While we stood in the playground, she had Nicky by the collar and was beating it for all her worth. She looked like a deranged woman, going mad. I don't know if she was trying to gain our respect but certainly after that we thought even less of her as a person of the religious cloth. Outside of the orphanage, everywhere Bridie was, Nicky the dog was with her. One day when Bridie had headed down the road to school, Nicky followed her and half way down the road he ran across the road, was hit by a car and killed. When Bridie heard about it she ran out of school, up the road and went crazy, screaming at the roadside. It took a long time before she got over the loss of her pet dog.

There is a particular day in my life that I shall never forget about. Bridie asked me to go with her to the glass house where old men sat during the day to while the time away. It was situated at the other side of the long corridor that we scrubbed every week. Bridie said that they would give us sweets and as a 10 or 11 year old I was tempted but hesitant. Bridie persuaded me and off we went, hoping we wouldn't meet any of the nuns on the way.

On arrival I was uncomfortable but being with Bridie I thought I was fine. The place smelt of pipe smoke and plants were laid out on a long table. At the end of this table was an old man sitting in the corner beckoning us to come for sweets. I seem to remember that there was another old man at the other side of the table. "Come on Marie", said Bridie as she tugged at my pinafore. I was reluctant to move any closer and kept thinking, if we are caught here away from the children's department we'll be killed. "We have to get back Bridie", I answered but my voice was barely a whisper. "Come here love," said the man, "I have some sweets for you." As I neared him, he suddenly pulled me towards him and gripped my wrist tightly in his huge hand. At that point my little body was engulfed with fear and the old man used his other hand to grope at my clothes until he eventually had his hand inside my pants. My mouth opened but nothing happened until something overcame me and without a flicker of thought I squeezed my tiny hand from his grip and ran out of that glass house as fast as I could.

I ran panting the whole way back to the children's department, hoping that Bridie was following me. I wanted to be as far away as possible from the old man, knowing what he did wasn't nice but I was also terrified he would tell the nuns I was there. I ran to the bathroom, locked myself in the toilet and cried for what seemed like hours. I eventually heard the sound of other children coming, so I came out and followed them to the dinning room for supper.

I had many sleepless nights thinking of what the old man did and would see him every day when went to the Chapel, as the old men and women sat at one side of the church while we children sat at the other side. I never made eye contact with him in case he shouted out that I was up at the glass house. As time past I pushed the horrible memory of that day to the recesses of my mind.

Back to Christmas, before the holidays started all the departments within the orphanage had to be scrubbed from top to bottom. Halls, landings, dormitories, dinning-room, bathrooms, classrooms and of course the Chapel, which took days to do. At Christmas the Chapel had to be spotless. There were two old sisters who took charge of the Chapel and I hated cleaning it because they examined every nook and cranny of the place and if it didn't satisfy the sisters then we had to do it all over again. We had to get in between the actual pews to wax them and our knees were so painful by the time we were finished. All this was done in preparation for all the Masses we had to attend over Christmas. We also had to get up for the midnight Mass at 11.00 pm, which lasted for well over an hour and again on Christmas morning when lots of us used to fall asleep. If you fell asleep, Sister Elizabeth would wake you by pulling your hair at the back of your neck or by nipping you under the arm.

Breakfast consisted of a fry, which was a real treat from the lumpy or runny porridge. Christmas day was the only time you got brown or red sauce. At dinner time there was an apple and orange on your table and in the afternoon we gathered in the large hall to await Santa coming. It was great fun. I used to wish Christmas was every day and believed in Santa until I was at least 11 years old. However, this wonderful belief was shattered one particular day, when I happened to walk into the Sister Maura's classroom and saw the true identity of our famous Santa Claus. Standing in front of me half dressed was none other than our handyman, Paddy. I stared for a few seconds before scurrying out of the room while not a word passed between us. I didn't tell any of the other girls, as I didn't want to spoil their belief. He came into the hall and as we lined up he handed us a Christmas present, but somehow it wasn't the same for me because of what I had discovered. Strangely enough in all the years we got presents in the orphanage and from the Belfast companies, I don't remember playing with any of the toys. I just don't know what happened to them.

Paddy had worked in the orphanage for as long as I

had ever known. He was well liked by both the nuns and children. He was a tall man with receding hair and was quite quiet. We were just used to seeing him working about the place. One day Carol was sent to work in the kitchen and while washing the pots and pans Paddy suddenly had a seizure and began wandering about the room like somebody lost. He appeared to be following Carol so she got very frightened and headed for the open window, jumped out and ran as fast as her wee legs could to the classroom. She burst into the room to Sister Elizabeth screaming that Paddy was doing strange things. Sister Elizabeth ran up to the kitchen and discovered poor Paddy lying on the floor and was able to get him help. He was married with children and sadly died in the late 80s.

Children from Nazareth House in Derry came up each Christmas to entertain the nuns and priests, while we were often sent to bed. One of the dormitories was above the concert hall, so we would gather round and lie face down with our ears to the polished floor, listening to the singing and music from below. It was great fun and in many respects better than attending the concert, because we were getting up to mischief and got away with it. On those occasions it didn't matter what we got up to as long as we were out of sight. Some of the older girls were allowed to the concerts and we would watch them going down the stairs with their new outfits on. When the cat's away the mice will play and we certainly did with no nuns or older girls to shout at us. After the concert the guests had tea and buns and we were the ones called on to clean up afterwards. There were many volunteers for this because there were always buns and sandwiches left over so we had a field day! The concert went on for about three evenings.

In 1959 we started going out to local families for two weeks over the summer period. A few girls at a time were sent to the sewing room, fitted out in summer dresses and given a tiny case containing some clothes. During my first time outside of the orphanage, I was taken by car to Mr and Mrs Campbell in Lurgan by Mrs Nelson. Instead of it being an exciting time I was actually very frightened. Everything beyond the orphanage was so strange.

The drive seemed to take forever with no conversation between us, for which I was quite happy about. Throughout the journey I stared at every building, garden, trees and the people we passed by in amazement. I was just captivated with everything in front of me and went into my own little world for what seemed like days until the car suddenly came to a halt. Sitting bolt upright, I glanced out the window to my right and noticed that we had stopped at a tiny cottage in the middle of nowhere.

At this point fear took over and I realised that I was going to be with these strangers for some weeks. Mrs Nelson opened the car door for me to get out but I just sat there staring at her, trying to tell her with my body language what I was feeling. "Come out", she said sharply and that was the last she spoke to me. Looking past her I could see a couple standing at the door of this tiny cottage, both smiling from ear to ear. I walked behind Mrs Nelson, who spoke to the couple but I couldn't hear what was said as my thoughts were elsewhere. "Come in pet", the lady said softly, almost with a whisper.

On entering the cottage I felt so closed in compared to the huge orphanage and looked all around me for other children, but there were none to be seen. However, by the time the holiday was over that didn't matter. That was the start of a wonderful holiday with the Campbells, whose kindness shown to me was just remarkable. I was very timid and scared to even speak, thinking about the Sundays we had walked for miles up and down the Ormeau and Ravenhill Roads and were told not to speak to strangers. To me this was no exception.

On the first day all I thought of was going to bed and these people not knowing that I wet the bed. What's going to happen if I do? I thought. That night I was taken into a beautifully decorated bedroom with a huge bed. To think that I was going to sleep in this lovely bed and then wet it was terrifying to say the least. I lay awake for hours thinking if I didn't sleep, then I wouldn't have an accident. Sleep did take over because next I woke to the smell of cooking and felt cold! The bed was wet! I froze on the spot thinking, what to do next. My fearful thoughts were interrupted by a voice saying, "Marie pet, come and have your breakfast." I just lay there and again heard, "Come Marie pet, your breakfast is ready." I eventually got myself dressed and opened the door very gently. "Come along, don't be frightened", she called. I was fearful of Mrs Campbell scolding me and telling me to wash the sheets out but I needn't have worried another minute because each night I went to bed it had been freshly made with not a word said on that matter.

At the back of the cottage the Campbells had a goat, which was chained to a hedge, and a dog. Every time I needed to use the toilet, which in those days was outside, it meant passing these animals so Mrs Campbell had to escort me each time. Regrettably being on my own made it very lonely and I fretted for my friends. Everything about that first ever holiday and the couple was so magical yet surreal.

The day Mrs Nelson collected me to return to the orphanage, part of me didn't want to go back yet strangely enough part of me wanted to return to where all my friends were. I had missed them more than anything else. Needless to say that was the last time I saw Mr and Mrs Campbell.

The following year two girls older than me went to the Campbell's. I was sent with two sisters to a family in Castlewellan. Both sisters were very cute with fair hair and deep blue eyes. Agnes had a speech impediment and often teased by other girls in the orphanage but she could easily stand up for herself. Her sister Cara was about two years older, tall, with lovely long thick fair hair. She always got on well with the nuns although wouldn't have been classed as one of their pets.

Again it was Mrs Nelson who drove us to Castlewellan. She worked for the nuns and if children needed to be taken anywhere she was called upon by Sister Luke. In fact Mrs Nelson's own children attended the primary school within the orphanage. On arrival, the three of us were taken into a large parlour-like room. The family had seven or eight children of their own at the time. Yet they took the time to take three of us from an orphanage. Just like Mr and Mrs Campbell, Dr and Mrs Moore were also very kind. This time I was with friends from the orphanage so I wasn't as frightened and felt much more comfortable but not regarding the bed-wetting because now I had the worry of being nicknamed. We were standing in the room when Mrs Moore asked, "Who needs the plastic cover on their bed?" I wanted to hide at that point and felt so embarrassed, when Agnes shouted out, "Oh Marie wets the bed!" All eyes were on me. She's going to send me back to the orphanage, I thought but thankfully, that didn't happen. Instead a large plastic cover was put on my bed and I had to lie on the bottom bunk bed to my disappointment.

We settled well with the Moore family but Agnes and Cara got on much better with the children than I did as I was still quite shy and timid. Mrs Hanna was a local lady who came in to help every day. She was a short, stout lady who was always smiling and jolly with us all. One day we were standing listening to Mrs Hanna chatting and I placed my hand on top of what I thought was a table, when Mrs Hanna shouted, "Merciful God, child, what have you done? Oh my God, child you have burnt your wee hand!" As she ran over to me, still talking, I pulled my hand back and felt a terrible pain. Never having seen a stove before, I had placed my hand on it and burnt myself. For fear of the repercussions I didn't even shed a tear. Mrs Hanna ran for Dr Moore, who came from his surgery and put some kind of cream on my skin. Instead of punishment I was shown gentleness and kindness, which I certainly wasn't used to.

We were made to feel so important to this family and had a lovely holiday that we would never forget. The three of us were sent back the following year and had as wonderful a time as the first. But as they say, all good things come to an end, and the holidays with families stopped in 1961.

In 1960 I began attending a special school for the educationally subnormal. It was to have a profound effect on me while in the orphanage and would continue for many years after I left. I started the new school term with the other girls from the orphanage and was settling in quite well, making new school friends. One evening I arrived home from school and after Sister Luke saw that we had our full uniforms on, she told me to go straight to the sewing room and see Sister Claire. Thinking that I was perhaps getting fitted with a new blouse, I headed off.

When I entered the room she had a new uniform and told me to put it on. I noticed that it was a navy tunic, with a different tie but it still had a white blouse. No questions were asked and nothing was explained. As I was coming out of the sewing room, Pat was going in. The following morning, while changing for school with my friends, Sister Luke shouted, "Why are you two madams still in this room?" All eyes were on Pat and myself but before I could respond, Sister Luke came right into my personal space, bent over me and said, "I hope you haven't missed that bus madam. If you have you will feel my hand, get out now!" That was my introduction to education at a school in Whiteabbey. It was a school for the educationally subnormal. I saw the girls waiting at the orphanage gates for the bus, so we joined them and shortly after that the bus arrived. This was the routine for the next five years.

When we arrived at the school there were other buses arriving too. The other children headed for their classrooms while Pat and I stood looking at each other, before somebody took us to the Head Nun's office. All eyes were on us and as Pat was black and I was swarthy some of the pupils asked if we were sisters! Pat was taken to one classroom and I to another. From that day I was branded backward. The school was a boarding school and was situated in beautiful grounds overlooking Belfast Lough. The only thing I enjoyed about the school was the scenery from the classroom window and I spent many days daydreaming and gazing out over the Lough. I also envied the boarders because they were so well treated. Although the teachers were lovely, I just switched off the day that Sister Luke sent me to Whiteabbey and lost all interest in learning.

Despite this lack of education I used to find ways of learning myself. The way I tried to teach myself to read was when Sister Elizabeth got the *Irish News* each evening. Once she had finished with it she left it lying on the table in the sitting room. I would wait until none of the girls were about and would look through the pages, trying to make sense of the words. I knew by trying to read the paper it would hopefully benefit me in the long term and reading the paper each day became my secret, as I was scared of being laughed at by my friends.

One day Sister Elizabeth gave some of the girls in our dormitory a little holy book called *The Saint Martins Magazine*. The girls she selected were allowed to pick pen pals to write too but I was excluded. Anyway I didn't really care, as I was afraid of being asked what school I attended. All I needed was somebody to recognise that I had something to give if only they would help and guide me. The one thing I did reasonably well in at school was physical education. I was even made prefect for a few years before leaving school.

When I was about 12 years old something very unusual happened. It was near Christmas time and we were all in the dinning room for our evening meal when Sister Elizabeth came over to me and said, "Marie, come with me." All eyes were on both of us as we left the room. She took me to the bathroom, told me to wash and even helped me, then ordered me to put a very pretty green dress on. I stared at the beautiful dress not believing that I, the orphan, was about to wear it. The excitement was overwhelming. Sister Elizabeth combed my hair and stood me back to make sure I was presentable. During the whole time I didn't say a word but thought to myself, "I must be going home." "Follow me," she said, setting off briskly. I followed her and not a word was said until we arrived at the door leading to the classroom. Sister Elizabeth stood behind me and with the door slightly ajar, she asked, "Who's that woman there?" I answered quickly, my voice shaking, "Please sister, I don't know." To which she replied sternly, "Go and speak to her, and find out who she is."

I walked nervously towards the lady and as I drew nearer I suddenly recognised who she was. She was Mrs McHugh, the first teacher who taught me at Whiteabbey. Imagine her coming to see me and giving me such a beautiful dress and a bag of sweets, I thought. In my innocence I didn't think to say thank you for the dress and sweets. "How are you Marie?" she asked nicely. "Ok," I said softly, knowing that Sister Elizabeth was in the next room listening. Mrs McHugh stayed a few minutes before saying, "Goodbye I will see you after Christmas Marie." As I watched her leave the room I was wishing she would take me with her. She was the first person to visit me in the orphanage. It wasn't until many years later that I was to learn who the dress actually came from.

When I returned to the other room, Sister Elizabeth was still standing there. "Who was that?" she asked. When I said that it was a teacher from Whiteabbey, she told me to go back to the other children. No sooner was the visit over than I was told to take the dress off and return it to the sewing room. It was never seen again.

As I was at a school for the educationally subnormal this meant I couldn't leave school until I was 16 years old. The girls at the secondary school left at 15 and once they had left they got transferred to the older girl's dormitory. They had the privilege of having a bit of privacy with a curtain surrounding their individual beds. I remained in the children's dormitory and hoped as soon as I left school I would be with my friends.

When I left school at 16, I didn't have an exam to my name. I was capable of achieving a goal but had no encouragement from the nuns. I was given the job of working with the young children, which I loved and was very happy caring for them. By this stage the younger ones weren't doing the scrubbing, waxing and polishing like we had done, which was great to see. Nevertheless, I could see my friends coming out of their dormitory and envied them. When I asked Sister Elizabeth if I could join my friends, I was ignored. It didn't take a genius to figure out why and I never got any further than the children's dormitory. After the girls left school and worked about the orphanage, they were given a half day off a month and some pocket money. When Sister Luke knew it was my day off she often found something for me to do and there wasn't anything I could do about it.

Loretta left the local secondary school at the same time as I left Whiteabbey and also worked with the children from her group. However, there was a big difference between Loretta and myself. She was very much liked by Sister Luke, who certainly didn't let me forget it. Loretta was very small for her age, had lovely brown curly hair and unlike me had come into the orphanage as a five year old. Her mother used to visit her quite often. She always had little baskets of sweets and tiny bottles of perfume, which we all wanted share of. Loretta's mother was very noticeable by her silky scarf she always wore around her head.

Loretta and I got on well, however, while the younger girls where at school I had to clean the dormitories, bathroom and was often up at the large kitchen peeling potatoes, while Loretta was given the easy jobs, like going for messages outside the orphanage. Sister Luke would send a child from her classroom to find me. When I would appear, she would say, "Get Loretta." Yet when we both came back to her, Loretta was asked politely to go on a certain errand, while I was left standing like a fool. Sister Luke would half close her eyes before saying, "You go about your business Madam." I just wasn't good enough in her eyes. Loretta was even sent to evening classes to learn office skills but I wasn't. The only thing I was fit for was cleaning. This nun did her utmost to degrade me in every way possible and did a very good job of bringing my self-esteem to an all time low. Self-worth and confidence simply didn't exist in my world. I often wondered what I had done to deserve this kind of existence. Was I being punished for the 'sin' of my mother?

I learnt to block out the nice things that could have happened to a child. The things that I couldn't forget were the things like attending a special school, having no parents, wetting the bed, having an alarm placed on my bed and being told I would be sent to a mental institution for breaking the shaft of a mop. I felt so worthless and, unfortunately, I wasn't the only one. What did these religious nuns know about the emotional, psychological, educational and physical well being of children? Did they even have any training to work with children? If so, what was their training all about? Crying out for affection and love wasn't asking much from these nuns was it? Good Christian Ireland had allowed women to enter a religious organisation where it was apparent that they were unhappy. Society, the Government and, most importantly of all, the Catholic Church had to know what way the orphanages were being run, yet they allowed children like me and many others to be treated in the manner in which we were. In my view nobody cared about the nuns so they didn't care about us. You know the old saying, not at my front door, why should I care.

We were never taken aside and told about our roots or where we came from, although some of the girls occasionally received visits. On one occasion one of my friends had a visitor who had given her a parcel for her birthday. After seeing Sister Elizabeth hand the parcel to my friend, I asked apprehensively, "Please sister when is my birthday?" "It's in February," she replied and swiftly left the room. I was about 9 or 10 years old at the time and looking at the joy on my friend's face at receiving sweets, I naively thought, "Maybe somebody will give me a parcel next February." In my innocence I thought the whole month was my birthday and it was many years before I realised that it was on a specific date.

No one ever told us about the facts of life either and puberty was a traumatic time for me. I found my changing body difficult to accept and was certain that I was becoming disfigured as punishment for my bed-wetting. I even hated taking part in physical education at school, which previously I had really enjoyed. I remember around this time I was being fitted with a dress in the sewing room, as we all did each summer and winter. It was much too small for me and while taking the dress off, my vest was riding up with it but I didn't want anyone to see my body. "What are you doing girly?" Sister Claire shouted, coming over to me and pulling the dress off, my vest coming off with it. Without thought I yelled, "That's my vest!" I was so humiliated at her leaving me exposed in front of other girls. It was bad enough seeing my body changing but to be shown to others in this manner was so embarrassing.

When I was about 12 or 13, a few of us were ordered

to carry some old school desks down from a very old out-building called the loft, where old furniture was stored, via a huge fire escape. These desks were made from cast iron and wood, and were quite heavy. While carrying the desks down the fire escape, the rusted iron steps collapsed. A desk fell on top of me and down I went the length of at least 20 steps. I lay there for a few seconds before realising what had happened. I instinctively jumped up and headed for the nearest toilet to examine my injuries. I saw a lot of blood and felt terrible pain in my groin. I remember being terrified because I had allowed the iron steps to collapse. I was cut quite badly but was scared to mention it to anybody. Nevertheless my friend Bridie told Sister Claire, who immediately ordered me to the sewing room.

When I entered Sister Claire took one look at me and demanded irritably, "Get the knickers off at once girly." I didn't want to take my pants off, so stood glaring at her in defiance. However, before I knew it, I being was dragged over to Sister Claire and to my total embarrassment had a dressing applied to the necessary parts. No sympathy was shown; I was just told to come back in a few days time to have the wound checked. I didn't return and to my relief, Sister Claire forgot about it. She often forgot the children's names and when she did want you it was, "Come here girly." But when she was in charge of us in the playground we really didn't mind because she wasn't as strict as the others.

The day I started to menstruate is one I shall always remember with sadness. I had noticed my body changing but couldn't understand what was happening. In fact I thought at one stage I was going to be disfigured for misbehaving. That was how I was. I had a dreadful day, feeling sick with tummy pains and a terrible headache. Just before tea time I disappeared to the bathroom and on seeing blood, thought I had cut myself without knowing it. I locked myself in the toilet remembering that dreadful day I had fallen from the loft and didn't want to go through that experience again. So I sat for some time crying and praying that the terrible pain would go away.

Some hours later an older girl called under the door of the toilet, "What's the matter with you Marie?" When I explained what was happening, she disappeared for a short time, before shoving something underneath the door, without telling me what it was. As I held this soft thing in my hand I thought it was something you wore on your head! This was a very traumatic time in my young life and my suffering could have been avoided if only the nuns had taken us aside and explained what exactly was happening. Some of the girls had been given a small book about purity to read. Sister Elizabeth would sneak out of her cell in the dead of night and shove a bulky item into a girl's bedside locker. It was done in such a secret manner it left me wondering what she was doing. Once again I was exempt because I wouldn't be able to read it and they felt I was incapable of comprehending what it was all about. Instead I had to learn the hard way.

As for boys, the only time we saw them was at Mass and of course beyond the yard leading to the laundry. On special Holy days a few boys were selected to come up to our orphanage to be Altar Boys during the Mass. Girls weren't allowed to be Altar Servers at that time. As soon as the Mass was over the boys had instructions to return to their orphanage and to speak to no one. It didn't matter if the boys had sisters in our place.

Making my first confession was another nightmare. While preparing us for our first confession, we were marched up to the Chapel on a Saturday evening and in very dim light were told to sit in the pews. An older girl called each of us in turn and ordered us individually to enter the confession box to reveal our so-called sins. As a seven year old, I hadn't a clue what the whole thing was about. Without any consideration or thought the older girl grabbed and shoved me into a very small, dark, creepy confessional box. Suddenly, I heard a man's voice come from nowhere. I thought the priest was God coming to get me for being bold. I almost fell over myself trying to get out of the box screaming, only to be pushed in again and again. That dreadful experience has haunted me to this day. My first communion holds also nothing but bad memories.

A few of us were often sent to the big kitchens at the weekends and I was one of them. We had to sit on a small wooden box and peel hundreds of potatoes from a huge tub. Afterwards we had to clean pots and pans in the large kitchen. When washing the pots and pans we needed to stand on a platform, as we were quite small. On one such occasion I vividly remember that I was washing away when I glanced out the kitchen window. I saw a poor person receiving a loaf of bread, a pound of butter and some tea. The poor looked so dishevelled and hungry that I always felt so sad for them, so it was very upsetting to watch. "I don't want to grow up," I heard myself saying aloud as I continued to stare at this poor woman, who was literally begging to survive. My thoughts were disturbed by the sound of the cooks coming into the kitchen and demanding the pots and pans.

Walking down the corridor to the children's department that evening I began to really think about what actually lay ahead for me. Believe me, I didn't relish the thought that I too would be begging to exist as an adult. The nuns were the only ones who knew what my fate was. They would decide where my future lay and to me that was terrifying. I realised that if Sister Luke had anything to do with it then the future wasn't going to be any better than the last 17 ½ years.

Everything changed in 1967, just as it had for the many girls before me. One day we are all together, then out of the blue some of the girls were gone, with no explanation as to where they were going. Many were never seen again. My day had started off as usual getting the younger ones up, dressed, off to the Chapel before breakfast and on to school. I had many duties to carry out, such as tidying the dormitory, bathroom and dinning room. That evening, shortly after teatime, I was summoned to the sewing room. "Girly, take that case and be at the parlour for 6.00 pm," Sister Claire announced. I stood staring from her to the case and fear began to build up inside me. That was the first hint that my days at the only place I knew from birth – cleaning, scrubbing, waxing, polishing and praying with all my orphan friends – was coming to an end. I was terrified. Without a word, I took the case and walked out of the sewing room for the very last time.

From that moment on nothing was ever the same again. When I got to the dormitory I opened the case, hoping to find the pretty green dress. To my horror all I saw was a night dress, one pair of knickers, a facecloth and carbolic soap. There was still nothing to say who I really was. I was panic-stricken and had flashbacks of the few happy and many sad days at the orphanage.

I was of no further use to the nuns. I was too old and they weren't short of workers, with girls coming up behind me to fill my gap. I felt very vulnerable and scared, with so many thoughts racing through my mind. Who on earth wants a wet the bed, educationally subnormal orphan? How was I going to explain to people beyond the orphanage who I was, when I didn't even know myself? Would I be ostracised on the outside just as I had been in the orphanage? I thought about the many days that I had sat precariously on the climber watching the 'outsiders' beyond the huge walls, which had hemmed me in for over 17 years. I was soon to discover that the outside world was to be an even harder place to survive in than the orphanage.

Seeing me holding a small brown case, the girls gathered round. "I am leaving here," I whispered to Ann as she sat on my bed, "I am going today at 6.00 pm and have to be up at the parlour. Mrs Nelson is taking me somewhere." "Oh Marie, we will miss you but I wish I was going with you," shouted Ann even before I had finished my sentence. Looking down at the bed I had slept in for many years, I thought, God it won't be empty for long.

Ann slept beside me in the dormitory. We used to talk at night, when lights were out, before Sister Elizabeth would shout out from her cell for us to be quiet. She was a year younger than me and we got on very well from the day she came into the orphanage as a nine year old, with her two sisters, Bernadette and Rosemary. She was quite small for her age, tubby, with black straight hair. I vividly remember the day she arrived. We were all in the sitting room watching the television, when Sister Elizabeth entered the room followed by three girls. Bernadette, the youngest, was eventually taken away to the nursery screaming. She was too young for our department. The scene was terrible, with all three girls screaming for each other and trying to get out of the room. Their brother was sent to the boys orphanage alone and we later heard that he continually ran away so they sent him to another orphanage in the country from which there was no escape.

When Ann and her sisters were taken into care, Ann, being the oldest, was in the house when their mother died. That was the last time she and her sisters saw any of her family. A few days later, Ann saw her mother's name stare out at her from the newspaper, which was lying on the table in the sitting room. She was never told about the mother's death by the nuns and didn't get to attend the funeral. Her mother was only 33 years old.

"Don't worry Ann, I will come back and see you all on Sundays," I replied softly, my voice shaking with fear, "How on God's earth will I cope Ann?" "Marie you will manage great, don't be frightened," my friend answered confidently. "I am really worried about the bed-wetting and if the people ask who I am," I said, welling up with tears. "I am sure Sister Luke will tell whoever you are going to all about you Marie," she said sympathetically. The mention of Sister Luke made my skin crawl. I had a terrible feeling that she wouldn't have given the people a very good impression of me.

I said my goodbyes to my friends for the last time and walked out of the room. I left the children's department and walked along the huge hall I had scrubbed and polished every Friday. Part of me was wishing I could be scrubbing it again rather than facing the unknown future. It was a horrible feeling and as I continued to walk, the sounds of children's voices began to fade before silence took over. I reached the parlour and stood alone for some time. Looking around the room, I realised it was another place that I wouldn't be waxing and polishing again.

My thoughts were interrupted by Mrs Nelson's voice, "Marie, are you ready?" Without answering I followed her like a little child, with my small case in hand. There was no nun to say, "Good luck for the future Marie." As far as they were concerned I was just a waste of space and someone to dispose of. That is exactly how I felt at that moment.

We headed towards the gates of the orphanage in which I had been abandoned and I was being abandoned again. I didn't even have a piece of documentation to say who I was or where I came from and was leaving without that knowledge. As we passed the kitchens from which I had watched the poor woman getting a loaf of bread, my heart sank. I wondered how long it would be before I would be doing the same!

I looked straight ahead and didn't turn back. There was nobody to look back at. I climbed into Mrs Nelson's car and didn't utter a word, just like my nine year old self going out on my first holiday. As the car moved off I glanced back at the building that had been my security and shelter for the past 17 years. There was nobody watching out for me, even from the dormitory windows. It was as if I didn't exist anymore. It wasn't long before the orphanage faded into the distance, taking with it my friends and the only life I had ever known.

Chapter Two

THE REAL WORLD

I SAT STARING OUT at the small narrow streets of Belfast, watching children playing in the side streets and people going about their business. I could be going anywhere and nobody really cares, I thought, with tears running down my face. We travelled for some time before Mrs Nelson's car turned off the main road and into a large driveway. At the end of the driveway was quite a big house, although no match for the huge orphanage I had just left.

"Come along dear," Mrs Nelson said, as I gathered my precious belongings. I stood behind her like a frightened pup as she rang the doorbell. After several rings the door was opened by a tall, well-dressed lady. She had dark, curly hair and appeared to be in her forties. "Do come in please," she said loudly with a broad smile on her face, "I am Mrs Burn." I was ushered into a room that looked similar to our parlours but slightly smaller. Mrs Burn and Mrs Nelson talked for a while but even though I was standing next to them, I didn't hear a word they said. I suddenly realised Mrs Burn was addressing me, "You come with me and I will show you your room Marie and when you have unpacked, come down to the kitchen." When I turned to follow her, Mrs Nelson was already rushing out the front door. Both women whispered to each other briefly, as if I wasn't there, then Mrs Nelson was gone and I was left with this stranger.

"Go to the very top Marie and you will see an attic," Mrs Burn said. I had never heard of an attic but headed for the top of the building until I could go no further. I came to a small, neat room that was quite cold. I didn't mind being at the top of the house, as I wanted to be out of sight, because of my problem. I quickly peeped under the bedclothes to see if there was a plastic sheet on the bed and thanked God that there was. I sat on the stool at the window for a moment and looked out at my new surroundings, wondering what lay ahead for me and how long I would be here.

I hurriedly unpacked and headed downstairs. "Oh there you are Marie," Mrs Burn said, as I got to the end of the stairs. I followed her to the kitchen where she told me to sit down and have a cup of tea that she had made for us. I was afraid to move or even make eye contact with this stranger in case I looked silly. As I drank the tea nervously, Mrs Burn took the opportunity of explaining my duties. The large house that was now my home was in fact a guest house with lots of bedrooms, three bathrooms and a big dinning room. The list of duties was so long, I wondered how I was going to cope and how on earth I would waken for 6.30 am without the sound of the bell in the orphanage. As if the lady had read my mind, she announced, "I will rap your door in the morning."

The following morning I was awake long before the Mrs Burn had a chance to rap my door. My bed-wetting of course continued and each morning I would dash down to the bathroom, rinse the sheets out and leave them in the washroom. A few days later Mrs Burn informed me that the sheets should be placed in the washing machine. I had never seen a washing machine and asked her to show it to me. I felt so inadequate.

My duties included cleaning the bathrooms, stairs, dinning room and of course the many bedrooms. The bedrooms had to be cleaned for a certain time because guests were coming and going. This kind of life was completely new to me and I found it difficult. The only night I didn't sleep was the first night but after that I was so exhausted I slept right through. Some days I wasn't finished work until well after 10.00 pm.

Initially I was treated fairly well and I even had my meals with Mrs Burn's family. However, it wasn't to last. After just a few weeks, Mrs Burn called me into the kitchen and announced, "Marie you must have your meals in the back kitchen from now on." This was the start of my segregation from them and the rest of society. The outside world wasn't what I had hoped for and unfortunately things went down hill from then on. I was experiencing first hand how people treated you when they knew you came from an orphanage.

I was there to work and to be used to Mrs Burn's advantage, and it was really no different to the nuns. I wasn't even allowed to associate myself with her three children, two boys and one girl. Nevertheless, that didn't stop me trying to communicate with their youngest child, who was blind and I felt a great empathy towards. I would let him touch my face while chatting and loved playing with him but his mother didn't like this. Again it didn't last as he was sent away to a special boarding school and that was the last I saw of him.

I was now in a world of silence and work, and the family's attitude towards me left me feeling worthless and ashamed. Not once did I hear from the nuns. No one seemed to care how I was getting on or even if I was dead or alive, out of sight out of mind, I suppose. I knew no one and had no freedom, and sadly my promise to Ann was broken through no fault of my own. I don't remember ever being paid and only had Sunday off, so I just stayed in my room crying for a better existence.

My only outing was to Mass and on the first Sunday I headed off alone and walked for what seemed like miles. I noticed people with hats and prayer books going into a large building, so I followed them. While sitting in the pew I gazed around thinking that the Chapel within the orphanage was so different from the ones on the outside. I attended the services for the rest of my time with this family and years later learnt it was a Protestant church. It never did me any harm! In fact I didn't know there was a difference in religions. I assumed the whole world was Catholic!

I was the only girl employed by the family so had to become Jack-of-all-trades. One day, things were running behind and Mrs Burn asked me to help cook the breakfast. I didn't tell her that I couldn't cook so headed for the kitchen to cook the breakfast for about 18 guests. I couldn't even fry an egg! I proceeded to heat the frying pan and threw the eggs into the heated oil, along with sausages and bacon. Things began to get rather steamed up in the kitchen and eventually, after some time and a lot of smoke, Mrs Burn appeared and screamed at the top of her voice, "Holy God, what on earth are you doing girl? Are you trying to burn the damn house down you stupid girl?!" Her voice made me jump, as I hadn't seen her enter the smoke-filled room. Everything I had in my hand went up in the air before landing on the floor. I just stared at her until she shouted, "Get out of the kitchen at once!" I bolted for the attic and cried. I was never asked to cook again to my delight but the cleaning increased.

Another incident had occurred a few days beforehand. I was tidying out the store under the stairs when I noticed a little toy machine gun. A little boy who was visiting from another country happened to pass and of course I lifted the toy out of the store and pretended to play with him, but to my horror he screamed at the top of his little voice and ran off to his parents. Without further ado I shoved the gun back in the store and pretended I knew nothing about it!

As time went on, I was spoken to less and less by everyone in the household, apart from when jobs had to be carried out. Eventually even the children snubbed me and I felt very inadequate and alone. I became so exhausted that I lost weight and even my menstrual cycle stopped. I was taken to the Doctor who asked if I was pregnant. I hadn't a clue what he was talking about and just answered "no".

Months passed and things weren't getting any easier. I had taken enough from these rich people so made the decision to leave the house while Mrs Burn was taking her children to school. I saw little of Mr Burn, as he was away from the early hours of the morning, so knew he wouldn't be around. I got up at my usual time of 5.30 am and started my cleaning. When Mrs Burn left with her precious children, I ran up to my room, collected the small brown case that I had arrived with and calmly walked away from that guest house, never to return. Many worries ran through my mind: Where the heck was I going to now? And what will happen when she eventually discovers I'm gone and reports it to Sister Luke? But my escape had started and there was no turning back.

Once out on the main road, blind panic set in as I watched the hustle and bustle of the traffic and people. At least they know where they are going, I thought, as I edged my way down the road. I walked for what seemed like hours and was too scared to ask anyone for directions in case they asked me where I had come from and who I was. Luckily the weather wasn't too bad and I saw different signs on the way. One sign said 'Kircubbin', which was familiar to me as that was where the boys from Nazareth Lodge went once the reached 11 years old. I heard bad reports about Kircubbin from girls who had brothers there, so I wandered on.

Relief took over when I saw a sign for Belfast and the first few miles after that were quite pleasant, as I enjoyed the scenic views. However, as time passed I became tired and hungry. I passed Scrabo Tower and Stormont Buildings before eventually arriving in Belfast exhausted. Most of my journey was spent contemplating where I was going to get food, shelter and money.

I knew some of the older girls who had left the orphanage lived together in a flat in Donegall Pass and that was my destination. I hoped my friends would help me and knew they wouldn't report me to Sister Luke. My feet were aching now and once in the centre of the town I plucked up the courage to ask somebody where Donegall Pass was. A young couple directed me in the right direction and off I went again. I eventually found the street the girls lived in and knocked on a few doors before an elderly lady pointed to the flat. What a relief.

When the door was answered Angela, one of the older girls, was standing there. She gaped at me in surprise and said, "My God, Marie what are you doing here?" "Please let me stay until I get somewhere else to live,"

I blurted out, nearly crying, "I hated that guest house!" "Why didn't you get a bus?" she asked. "Sure I have no money and hadn't booked one," I replied sharply. She started laughing, "You don't have to book a bus, you just get on at the bus stop and pay once you board it." I found myself begging her to let me in, before she opened the door wide enough for me to squeeze past. Angela was very attractive and seemed to get even more attractive as she got older. She had very swarthy skin and kept herself to herself in the orphanage. She later went to work in a photographers firm and did quite well.

When she brought me into the sitting room it was full of girls, some I knew, some I didn't. "It's okay Marie has run away from her job," she announced. Mary got up from her seat and headed towards the kitchen saying, "I suppose you can stay for a wee while but we don't really have the room." At that point all I wanted to do was sit down and have something to eat. "I'll leave as soon as possible," I said, sitting down on her seat. Thankfully the other girls in the flat agreed to me staying. I slept on the floor of the bedroom because there were so many in the flat that it was two to a bed already.

My stay in the flat wasn't easy, as during the day the girls were out working and I was just sitting about, which was soul destroying. I didn't know how to look for work and was starving because there wasn't much food in the flat. Even at this point of my life I was still bed-wetting, which made some of the girls quite angry and there were arguments between us. However, I was grateful to have a roof over my head, all be it for a short time.

I was with the girls for a few days, when Loretta called at the flat to tell me that Mrs Burn had contacted Sister Luke. Immediately all the bad memories of Sister Luke came rushing back, particularly the day she threatened to send me to Muckamore Abbey for breaking the mop. "Marie Sister Elizabeth wants you to come to the orphanage," she said. At first I resented returning to the establishment where I was only known for my backwardness and bed-wetting, "No way Loretta, they'll kill me for running away from those people." Loretta called twice more, and on the third attempt said, "Marie, Sister said that it doesn't matter what time you come back, she will wait up for you." I couldn't believe what I was hearing. "It's Mrs Burn's word against mine, who was going to listen to my reasons for leaving?" I asked Loretta, but said I'd think about it.

I spent most of the day in deep thought, considering my options and by nightfall I really was hungry and mentally exhausted from all that had happened over the past few days. Around 11.00 pm I finally decided to return to the orphanage and headed off towards the Ormeau Road, actually trembling at what lay ahead. I was about to take Sister Elizabeth's at her word.

By the time I had reached the huge gates of the orphanage it was almost midnight. Holding the now familiar suitcase in my hand, I reached up to the bell and the sound of it echoed in my ear, which jolted me. "My God this bell would waken the dead," I said loudly, as though speaking to somebody. I waited for what seemed like ages until eventually I heard the rattle of keys from the other side of the gate. The gate opened and to my amazement none other than Sister Elizabeth stood looking at me. I tried to open with mouth, trembling with fear, but she got in first, "Go up to the dormitory, there's a bed for you." That was the only sentence said. I passed her with my head down and walked down the same long corridor, up the stairs and landings that I had cleaned for years. Without further ado I entered the dormitory and upon seeing one bed vacant in the corner, I headed straight for it. At this stage nothing else mattered but food and sleep. Sitting on the side locker was a plate of bread and jam and a glass of milk – I couldn't believe my eyes.

As I climbed into the bed she said in a whisper, "I didn't hear anything." Then she was gone. I certainly wasn't going to say a word because I was so scared of what she would do. Before drifting off to sleep, I glanced around the dormitory and could see some of my friends were still there.

I woke early the following morning and thought of the unusual kindness shown to me by this nun. When the rest of the children saw me in the dormitory they all wanted to know why I was back. I told them that I hated the place the nuns sent me to and that I had run away. We went to Mass and all the old memories flooded back to me as

I looked around the Chapel. To my surprise I didn't see the old man from the glass house and never saw him again. I wondered if he had left. During the day, Sister Elizabeth sent for me. "Mrs Burn contacted us when you left. I am not going to go any further with this issue. You can continue to look after the wee ones," she said and the subject was never mentioned again.

Despite not wanting to be back in the orphanage again it was better than struggling in the outside world. I'd seen how cruel the real world could be. I was delighted to be given the job of caring for the wee ones and that was what I focused on. I encountered Sister Luke on a few occasions but was ignored as usual unless it was to do with cleaning and she made sure that I wasn't excluded from any form of physical hard work.

Months went by and just as it happened the first time, I was sent to the sewing room for a suitcase. Believe it or not, the same brown suitcase was sitting on the floor waiting for me, as if it had never been opened since my return. I was told to report to Sister Elizabeth, who explained, "Marie there is a couple in South Belfast looking for another lodger, so come up to the parlour for 6.00 pm this evening." "Not again", I thought. Sister Elizabeth continued, "Agnes is already there so you will be company for each other."

I explained to the younger ones that I was leaving and could tell they were upset, as some of them cried. "I will miss you all but hope it works out for me this time," I told them as I cleared what little belongings I had from my bedside locker. There was some consolation knowing that I was at least going to be with Agnes. Saying my goodbyes to my friends for the second time, I headed to the parlour and sat alone for an hour until a nun opened the door and said, "Go out to the front gate." As I walked alone towards the gate blind panic set in as I thought of my first dreadful encounter. I was soon to discover my experience in the guest house was just a taste of what lay ahead.

Chapter Three

AN INNOCENT RELEASED

I LEFT THE ORPHANAGE in much the same manner as the last time. There was no nun to see me off and no piece of paper to tell me who I really was. That was still my biggest concern, knowing my identity and where I came from. As I passed the old gate lodge, where the poor collected their food, I quickened by step. I noticed a car with a man and woman sitting in it and the woman beckoned me over. She shouted, "Hello Marie", as I climbed into the backseat but I didn't respond or utter a word throughout our journey, choosing instead to stare out the window.

During the drive, the man kept looking at me in the mirror, which made me feel very uncomfortable. He was quite thin, with a very solemn expression and was wearing a dirty boiler suit. The woman appeared to be quite the opposite. She was very short and fat, wore glasses and looked friendly enough. The journey wasn't as long as the first time, in fact it was no time until we arrived in a long street off the Lisburn Road in Belfast.

Compared to the guest house, this house was very small and was one of a long row of two up, two down parlour houses. The house had a tiny garden with a few plants and a nice rose bush, which was surrounded by railings. I got out of the car, stood looking around me and thought, what now? "Come on Marie. This is where you will be living", the woman announced in a jolly voice. I followed her into the house without answering. On entering I noticed how just how tiny the place was. It had a little kitchen, sitting room, parlour and two bedrooms. There was no bathroom and the toilet was outside in a tiny enclosed yard. I felt completely hemmed in.

"Sit down love", the woman said in her strong Belfast accent as we entered the sitting room. I sat on the seat at the window, which overlooked the poky, unkempt yard. Some minutes later I heard a familiar voice, "Hi Marie." It was Agnes and God was I glad to see her. "What's it like here?" I whispered but before she could respond the woman came into the room from the kitchen. "Don't be afraid love. You can call me Jean," she announced, "You will be sharing the room with Agnes, Marie." I noticed she appeared quite breathless as she spoke. I couldn't understand why, as she hadn't been rushing. I was also aware that she appeared to hover around us all the time, not really giving us our own space. Perhaps this is normal, I thought.

A few days later Agnes said she was going to the pictures. I wanted to go with her but had no money. Jean tried to stop her going out but Agnes was defiant and went anyway. I didn't want to sit with these strangers on my own, so headed off to bed early and cried myself to sleep. I just felt so lonely.

Some time later I was wakened by terrible noises coming from downstairs and realised it was Jean shouting at Agnes. I came out of the bedroom and sat on the top of the stairs listening to the two of them arguing, but most of the uproar was coming from Jean. More arguments followed in the coming days and it let me see another side to this lady that I was now lodging with. In the following days and weeks the atmosphere between Jean and Agnes was terrible. The only time Agnes and I could get talking in peace was in the comfort of the bedroom we shared. Jean reminded me of Mary Anne in the orphanage, snooping around and appearing out of nowhere unexpectedly. With the house being so small there really was nowhere to hide and little room for privacy.

As time passed, the rows got worse between Agnes and Jean. "Yous are suppose to be here to help us," I heard her shout with venom in her voice, "and if you don't like it here then you can get out." I simply stared at Agnes, hoping she didn't hear the last statement but Agnes had heard her very clearly. "Sure I'll go and will find a better place than this one, that's for sure," Agnes retorted, running straight out of the sitting room to the bedroom, with me in tow. "Jesus, Agnes, you don't mean it do you?" I pleaded, running up the stairs behind her. "I couldn't stay with that woman another day," she answered, her voice quivering, "she's told me to go and I am going. She isn't going to ruin my life and dictate to me when to sit, stand, eat and work. We had enough of that in Nazareth House." She went on to say, "I had planned to meet a friend tonight at the pictures and won't be back, I am sorry Marie." I gazed at her wanting to say, "My God, take me with you" but the words wouldn't leave my mouth. I just froze. I had replaced Agnes's sister Cara, who had also left the house some weeks earlier in the same manner but I didn't know that. Now Agnes was going and I was going to be left with these people that I wasn't particularly happy with.

While Agnes packed her few possessions, Jean entered the room like a mad person, bawling at the top of her voice, "You can go to your bloody friends, and don't come back here! See how long they'll put up with you." All this was said in one breath by a person who was so breathless that I was waiting for her to collapse. I was terrified.

As Agnes continued to pack her few items I followed her like a puppy, begging, "Don't go Agnes, I don't want to be here on my own." "I am not staying here another minute with that crazy woman. We can't even have a social life Marie," she said. Jean stood at the door as though to block Agnes's exit. "Come with me Marie," Agnes said softly. I wanted to go so much but something in my head was stopping me. I kept thinking that if Sister Luke found out that I had left another place, I would definitely be sent away. I was still standing as Agnes passed me, went down the stairs, out the door and turned to me to say, "See you some time Marie." I stood like a frightened child as Agnes left the house for the last time. I wanted to kick myself, here was an opportunity for me to go with Agnes and I didn't take it. Even today I don't know why I didn't leave.

By now it was 1967 and I got a job in a local stitching factory on the Donegal Road called the Star Factory. After a few weeks Teresa arrived. She was a year younger than me and we had been in the same dormitory in the orphanage. We had always got on well. She had lovely long fair hair, was quite attractive, quiet and very smart. While in the orphanage she was picked to go to most of the Christmas parties and learnt to play the violin. A man used to come every Saturday and only a few of the girls were chosen to have lessons. Needless to say I wasn't one of the lucky ones, yet even as a child I loved music.

Teresa had a strong personality and was very much her own person. She spent a lot of time reading when not working in the local box factory. As far as Teresa was concerned, she was there as a lodger and nothing else and unfortunately this didn't suit Jean.

In Teresa's case Jean didn't get the chance to throw her out, she just came in from work one evening and announced, "Marie I am leaving here at the weekend." I must be hearing things, I thought. Even as I watched Teresa pack her few things I couldn't pluck up the courage to go with her. It felt as though there was a magnet preventing me from moving away from the house. The following evening she left and never came back. I had now missed two chances to get away. I later heard that Agnes went to live in Scotland and Teresa went to America.

In the very early stages of living with Jean and Tommy, I used to visit the orphanage on a Sunday to see my old friends. We would catch up on the happenings within the orphanage and every time I visited there would be new faces, children I didn't know, who had come up from the nursery or from outside.

One day, when I was in the town, I saw a group of girls from the orphanage in the distance with Sister Luke. I ran towards them and as I got closer, I heard Sister Luke say loudly, as though she wanted me to hear, "Come along girls quickly now." She ushered the girls away from me and even when some of them saw me, she forced them to move on. I was left standing on the pavement like a complete fool.

I visited the orphanage a few more times after that until Jean and Sister Luke put a stop to it. On one of my last visits Ann told me that she had overheard Sister Luke speaking to Jean in the parlour one time, where Ann was working after leaving school. Sister Luke was sending another girl to lodge with her, and it turned out that girl was me.

One Sunday I was visiting, along with other older girls, and we were in the little sitting room playing records when Sister Luke came in. She turned the records off and announced, "It's time you lot were going and don't come back, you are coming up here too much." Sadly, that was the end of my visits to the only friends I had.

Now, let me tell you a bit more about the people I lodged with. Jean was born in a small terraced house in West Belfast in the early 20s and was the eldest of four children, three girls and one boy. Apparently her parents owned a small corner shop. Jean boasted that she did quite well at the junior school and was offered a place at the local grammar school but that she was taken out of school following the death of her father, who apparently died from consumption. She was now expected to find employment at the tender age of 12 to support the family financially. In those days nothing was thought of sending children out to work. Families were large and money was scarce. The little corner shop soon became a burden to the mother and eventually it was sold.

The only employment Jean could find was laundry work and this meant leaving the house at 6.00 am and not returning home until 8.00 pm each evening. She said that the damp conditions in the laundry caused her asthma and throughout the years her condition deteriorated. Her employers dismissed her due to her frequent asthmatic attacks and spells of hospitalisation.

Jean's sisters and brother managed to gain grammar school places and later found secure employment. Jean resented this and increasingly rowed with her mother until finally she ran away from home. She later met Tommy and shortly after that they married. She was 20 and Tommy was a few years older. According to her, Tommy hadn't done well at school, nor had he got on well with his family. She admitted that marriage provided security and an escape from all of her problems. They went to live on the Lisburn Road in South Belfast and Tommy found work as a road labourer but the pay wasn't great.

Not long after their marriage, Jean had to have a hysterectomy, which left her childless. I spent many years listening to them argue and Tommy would often cast it up to Jean for not having his children.

As the years passed Tommy and Jean decided to apply to the Good Shepherd Convent for a girl to lodge with them. A girl from the convent lived with them for some years but there were lots of problems with her and Jean. The girl continually ran away and Jean was always up at the Good Shepherd complaining. She actually told me this herself. After years of running to and fro the girl eventually went to Australia. Jean tried unsuccessfully to get her back by torturing the nuns. It was after this that they got girls from Nazareth House. I remember Ann telling me that Jean was never away from the place and that was the start of the couple being allowed to have girls from the orphanage stay in their home. All that mattered to the nuns was getting rid of another girl to make room for the younger ones coming up.

Initially I got on fine with Jean and Tommy, but I found their home quite a tense place to live. They argued a lot and this only increased the longer I lived there. One Thursday evening Tommy came home late from work. Jean had being standing out at the gate waiting for him, just as she did with me. God help us if we were a few minutes late. Anyway, Tommy came in and he was acting strangely, laughing and making silly comments. This wasn't like his usual quiet self and it made me quite uncomfortable, as did the odd smell surrounding him. I quickly learnt that this smell was alcohol.

From that day on, every Thursday at the same time Tommy arrived home in the same state, resulting in more terrible arguments. More times than enough Tommy would throw his dinner plate across the room, either because his dinner wasn't hot enough or there wasn't enough on the plate. Jean and Tommy's relationship was my first introduction to married life and I often thought, if this is what marriage is like then I don't want any part of it.

Regrettably, I also discovered there were many faces to Jean's character. She was very manipulative and controlling. Even though I had no medical knowledge, she seemed to use her asthma to her advantage, bringing on an attack at will. I always felt that something wasn't quite right with her mentally.

I was very lonely when Sister Luke stopped me visiting my friends at the orphanage, so I decided to go to a club on the Antrim Road, where some of the older girls met on a regular basis. I went once or twice and really enjoyed the company. I had a lot in common with the girls, even though most of them were much older than me. One night I was late coming home, as I had to wait for a lift from a lady who helped out at the club. Jean was standing at the gate waiting for me. I was now 18 years old and very embarrassed that my friend could see someone was waiting up for me, especially when I noticed her looking in her mirror as she drove away. "What time of the bloody night is this to be coming home? You have kept me out of bed waiting for you," Jean screeched in my face. "I was at the club and had to wait for a lift home," I answered quietly, as it was late and I knew she would have to have the last word. She seemed to enjoy arguing and getting her own way. I walked passed her and said nothing more. That was the last time I went to the club, Jean said money was scarce and there were bills to pay.

I continued to work in the factory, which I absolutely hated but at least it got me away from the house. The factory work was very hard, with ten minutes for tea break and half an hour for lunch. Everybody stayed for lunch but I had to go home because Jean complained that she needed me to do messages and by the time I got home from work particular shops would be closed. We were paid every Thursday and rain, hail or shine Jean would be standing outside the factory at lunchtime to collect my pay. I thought this was the norm but always wondered why the other workers weren't doing the same.

I still remember the feeling of achievement when I received my very first wage, but I never got to enjoy the profits. If I asked for money to live on, Jean's response was always the same, "You're supposed to hand in your wages because I have to feed and clothe you. Anyway Sister Luke told me to keep a good eye on you." She regularly used Sister Luke to play on my insecurities, "I don't know what you are moaning about, Sister Luke said you're a slow learner and had to be supervised at all times and also that you wouldn't be able to cope on your own." I was trapped and too afraid to run away again in case Sister Luke sent me to Muckamore Abbey. I lost count of the nights I cried myself to sleep but I had no option but to stay put and unfortunately Jean knew it.

I found out you could earn more money in the factory by working extra hours and in my innocence I told Jean this. Of course I ended up doing as much overtime as possible. You also got a bonus at the end of the week if you got into work before the expected time. One morning, after cleaning the house, I rushed down the road with the hope of getting in early. When I arrived at the factory I realised I had one shoe and one slipper on. Not getting that bonus infuriated Jean and led to another row.

I used to be very tried by the end of my factory shift but Jean also expected me to work when I returned to the house. I had cleaning to do and the animals to care for, as they had eight cats and two dogs. Jean said her asthma prevented her from walking the dogs but I didn't mind this duty so much as I liked the fresh air and it provided an escape each morning and night from listening to Jean ranting on about the silliest things.

One day I arrived home from work and Jean announced,

"I have a wee job for you Marie. It is a job cleaning offices after 6.00 pm for 2 hours." I tried to reason with her that I was really tired already but she interrupted, "For God's sake, we need the money to pay the bills." Here we go again, I thought and of course, she won the argument. I went from one tedious job to another and I was so exhausted that I found it very hard to focus at the factory.

I generally kept myself to myself when in work but some of the girls asked me out with them socially on several occasions. I was never able to go because Jean conveniently had an asthma attack or ended up in hospital. She had a awful way of making me feel guilty when she was in hospital and I was expected to visit her morning and evening. On one occasion I went to see her later than the visiting time, along with two of my friends. As we walked along the corridor to the ward, Jean met us halfway shouting, "Where the bloody hell where you!" As she spoke she pushed her finger right into my chest. I was terribly embarrassed and rather than make a scene, I simply introduced her to my friends, whom she barely looked at. It was no better when my friends called to the house for me. Jean sat in the parlour taking full control of the visit and it became so embarrassing that I actually wished nobody would call, which was of course what Jean wanted.

Over the Christmas period in 1967, Jean reluctantly allowed me to attend a party with the girls from the factory but warned me to come home early. While at the party I met a man who wanted to arrange a date with me.

At the age of 18 years this was my very first date and I was anxious. On the way home after the party I thought of all the ways to tell Jean that I had been asked out on a date. When I reached the house, of course she was waiting for me at the gate. "What time of the night is this to be coming home at?" she roared as though it was the middle of the day. "Keep you voice down. The whole street will hear you, its 1.00 am in the morning," I whispered. I knew what was coming, rows, rows and more rows, and they continued up in her bedroom.

I eventually announced, "I have a date at the end of the week." "And where the hell do you think you are meeting this man?" she interrupted, while Tommy lay in bed saying nothing. There was no way I would even consider bringing him or anybody else into this mad house, I thought to myself but instead I said, "For God's sake we are meeting at Clarke's Shop." I knew her reaction would be negative but when I told her that he worked in the Shipyard even I was horrified at her reaction. "Jesus Christ," she screeched, "he's a Protestant!" I didn't even know what a Protestant was, so I didn't answer her. I don't think it was the fact that the man was of a different religion that worried her though, it was the fear of me developing a good relationship and seeking freedom. She didn't want to lose her slave.

She went on about the date for days, until I got so fed up listening to her ranting on about it that I didn't go to Clarke's Shop. Because of her, my opportunity of meeting someone was destroyed. I often wondered if he ever turned up.

Work at the factory started to dry up as contracts were going to other countries offering cheaper rates. We were down to working only three days a week but one particular day I got up and pretended to go off to work as usual. I was actually meeting Loretta in Belfast City Centre, where she took me to one of the Government buildings to obtain my birth certificate. I had wanted to search for my roots since leaving the orphanage but it was something I needed to do on my own. I didn't want Jean to know that I had missed work in case she asked my why, so I worked enough overtime that week to ensure I earned my usual wage. Thankfully she was none the wiser.

As I poured over my birth certificate, Loretta explained that "Lots of girls go searching for their roots Marie." "Why didn't the nuns give us this information Loretta?" I asked. "Marie, I don't know that, sure they didn't tell us anything," she replied. I was stunned by what the piece of paper revealed: my name, my mother's name and her address. I had a flashback to the day that Sister Elizabeth said, "Don't be silly Marie. You don't have a mother." Yet this piece of paper was telling me differently. The information was mind boggling and I couldn't believe what I was seeing. I was going to make sure that nobody would ever take this information from me, so I read and digested the document until it was well and truly stored in my mind.

Chapter Four

THE BREAKDOWN

In 1968, while working in the Star Factory on the Donegal Road, something happened that changed my life drastically. I was working away at my sewing machine one afternoon when Mr Brown approached me, "Marie, turn off your machine and come with me to the boardroom please". I stared up at him and asked anxiously, "What do you want me for?" To which he simply replied, "Marie come with me please." I didn't respond but continued sewing until he reached across and turned the machine off.

I followed Mr Brown from the factory floor, feeling eyes on me from every direction. "Am I going to be sacked?" I asked but Mr Brown just walked on. On entering the boardroom I noticed a lady standing at the other end of the room. She was quite tall, had dark curly hair, and was wearing a fur coat and lots of jewellery. Realising that I didn't know this person, I turned to tell my boss, but he had already left the room.

I didn't know what was going on and was about to follow him out of the room when I heard the strange lady say, "Hello Marie, my name is Mrs White. I am here on behalf of your mother." Am I hearing things? I thought, staring at her totally bewildered. After a few seconds I slid into the nearest chair, whispering, "Did you say my mother?" There was brief silence before she continued, "Your mother came to Belfast on business and met someone and some months later you were born. However, because of circumstances your mother wasn't able to keep you, and for that reason, you were placed in an orphanage." "I don't believe what I am hearing," I said, my mind racing, "My God, Mr Brown is going to know all about me now." The shock and confusion made me feel physically sick and although I didn't want this stranger to see me cry, the tears were already streaming down my face.

The woman explained that she was a solicitor and when I looked her straight in the eye, I saw no compassion. I could tell that this was only a job for her and I am sure a well paid one at that. She wasn't worried about the effect this revelation was having on me.

"Are you telling me that I have a mother?" I blurted out, looking over at the door and naively thinking that the woman who brought me into this horrible world was about to enter. What a fool I was! "Why doesn't she come and tell me herself?" I asked but the solicitor merely responded, "I have to tell you that you will not be allowed to contact your mother, and if you want to know how she is keeping you can do so, but only through me." "Have you finished?" I interrupted, thinking in all the years of misery there was nobody to ask how I felt or what I wanted. "I have a lot of business to do and a long journey ahead of me," she declared and without asking me how I was, she walked past me to the door. As she opened the door she reached into her fancy handbag, turned to me and handed me a small picture, explaining, "I thought you'd like to have this for keepsake."

I waited until she had left the room before looking at the picture and saw a very pretty woman staring up at me. It sent shivers up my spine. So this was the person who had brought me into the world. I noticed the picture was wet from my tears, so I stood for few minutes to compose myself before leaving the room.

I walked back to my sewing machine in a daze, hearing Mr Brown call something to me that I didn't hear. I sat down, turned on the power and started my work again. Maura, who sat behind me shouted over the noise of the dozens of sewing machines, "Where were you Marie?" I didn't answer and after asking me a few more times she gave up.

The rest of the day was a total blur. The more I thought of the encounter with Mrs White, the angrier I became. That was the first and last time I saw her. On my way home that evening I was wondering how on earth this lady knew I worked in a factory and how she found me. I really was hoping that Jean had nothing to do with it and to my relief the encounter with the solicitor wasn't ever mentioned.

That Sunday I made my way to the orphanage hoping to find out if it was the nuns who had sent Mrs White to see me. While walking along the familiar corridor that I had scrubbed for years, I happened to meet Sister Elizabeth. "A lady called Mrs White came to see me at the factory during the week. Do you know who she is?" I asked. "Oh Rev Mother decided that your mother should know about you and that's all I know," she replied sharply and disappeared before I could ask anything more. After all, we never could ask questions! Sister Elizabeth's response was as cold as the solicitor's and since she was the same nun who told me as a child, "Don't be silly Marie. You don't have a mother", what else could I expect? The whole situation didn't make sense to me but I knew I wouldn't get any support from the Christian people who raised me. I simply wanted to run and hide from the cruel world.

As the days and months passed I tried so hard to put the visit from Mrs White to the back of my mind but I couldn't. I became quite mixed up psychologically and lost hope in everything and everybody. I just didn't care anymore and with no one to turn to for support, my mental state began to show physically. I lost quite a bit of weight and workers in the factory began commenting on it but I didn't care what people thought.

I received a letter from the solicitor a few weeks letter, delivered to the house. I was shocked that she knew where I was staying and never thought for one moment that I would hear from her again now Jean was involved. "Who would be sending you a letter?" Jean asked as she handed me the envelope. I was surprised she hadn't opened the damn thing. "Och just one of the girls," I replied, disappearing to my room with the letter.

Sadly, I was disappointed with what I read, as it merely said how nice it was to meet me, how her journey was and what the weather was like. That night I read the letter over and over again, hoping it would reveal something about my mother. After much thought I decided that I would play her at her own game. A few days later when Tommy and Jean went out, I got their writing pad and put pen to paper. I hadn't a clue where to start, as I had never written a letter before.

I wrote about silly things like my work, the weather and to tell my mother that I was asking for her, rather than writing down what I really wanted to say. There was so much I wanted to ask but I had no idea how to express myself nor how to communicate through a complete stranger. I was also terrified that Jean and Tommy would walk in at any minute. Jean had stamps and envelopes in the side cabinet, which I stole and quickly posted the letter before they got back. Running back from posting the letter, I suddenly realised that if a reply came, Jean would see it. Before that I had never received any mail and I wondered how I would explain it. I suddenly realised that somehow I didn't actually care.

A few days later I got a reply. Jean came rushing into the sitting room with an envelope raised high in the air, "Here's another letter, whose this from?" I quickly jumped up and grabbed the letter, "Oh that's from one of the girls in the orphanage again." She stood silent and motionless as I left the room. Sitting on top of my bed I opened the letter, which thankfully I was able to read. It was weird reading a letter sort of from my mother, but not directly from her. The letter was very short and Mrs White only wrote about the weather and her family, which I wasn't interested in. At the end she mentioned my mother only to say that she was well. I was disappointed that there was nothing more and a bit deflated.

By the end of 1968 I had received some jewellery on my birthday, Easter and at Christmas time. There was no indication if it was Mrs White or my mother sending the gifts. On a few occasions I desperately tried to gain information about my mother but Mrs White never fell for it.

Jean became suspicious and quizzed me about my letters and gifts. I told her nothing for months but eventually decided to explain to her and Tommy. I'm not sure why I thought they would understand, maybe I was just desperate for someone to help me find out more about my mother. Of course when I asked Jean would she help me find my roots, her face said it all. "See, Tommy! Didn't I tell you she was up to something? I knew those letters and gifts weren't from those girls in that orphanage," she screeched angrily. "Good God, I am only asking for your help, not your criticism!" I said, storming out of the room and banging the door, "Sorry I mentioned anything. I should have known what your reaction would be." I realised with sadness that I was behaving exactly like Jean. As I was heading up the stairs Jean stood at the bottom ranting on, "Hmm, I don't see why you want to trace your roots when they didn't want you. We let you lodge here, you should be grateful. That's the thanks we get Tommy!"

Despite Jean's objections I continued communicating with the solicitor. I was writing a letter in my room one day when Jean barged in without knocking on the door and demanded, "Are you not letting me see what you are writing?" "No I am not!" I retorted to which she replied in almost a whisper, "Sure Sister Luke said that you're backward so you wouldn't be able to spell." I knew she was egging for another row so I ignored her. The least said is the easiest mended.

In 1969 I received a letter from Mrs White that shocked me to the core. All the letters to date had been written in longhand, but this time the letter was typed. Even I, without an education, knew it was an official letter. It started off with the usual chat about the weather and my work, but as I continued my eyes fell on the sentence "Should anything ever happen to your mother and as her family don't know of your existence and probably never will, you will be no part of her will." I may have been educationally subnormal but I understood what it meant. The words "don't know of your existence" cut like a knife. "These aren't the words of a mother surely. Why would a mother relay such a letter to her daughter?" I cried out loudly in the empty room. My voice echoed through the stillness. I had no understanding of legal matters but the letter left me wondering why on God's earth they contacted me in the first place. I didn't reply to the letter and I really wouldn't have known how to. The ball was left in my court and I eventually wrote to Mrs White to say that all communication between us was to cease.

I didn't mention it to Jean, knowing it would be another feather in her cap but of course she didn't miss much. "I noticed you haven't been getting any mail lately," she remarked one day. Instead of just ignoring her I retorted, "No aren't you delighted?" "Oh Tommy did you hear that? And you can be sure that your mother is behind it all," she gloated. There was no point in responding as I hadn't a clue what she was getting at. With the knowledge that neither the solicitor nor the couple I was lodging with were prepared to help me in my quest for answers, I realised it was entirely up to me to take control of the situation. But how on earth was I going to change things?

I lost more weight and my health was getting worse by the day. Working in the factory during the day, cleaning offices at night, and being miserably unhappy was hugely draining my system. Life had nothing good to offer and I was screaming for help but nobody heard my cries. They say laugh and the world laughs with you but cry and you cry alone; and that was true in my case. In early 1969 I was eventually admitted to hospital where investigations were carried out to understand my extreme weight loss. Jean of course didn't help matters. She visited one evening and demanded, "Who is going to clean the offices; walk the dogs and look after us? We won't have any money coming in and that's your fault." Some of the patients in the bed near me heard everything but I didn't care.

A few days later a consultant came and sat on my bed. "Marie, we know that there is nothing physically wrong with you but you have a problem psychologically, which needs sorted our urgently," he explained, speaking softly, "I am sending you to another unit within the hospital grounds." I interrupted, "I am happy here don't send me home." I was taken back by his immediate response, "Where are your parents Marie?" Somehow I felt quite at ease with this doctor and answered him freely, "I don't know where they are." I found myself opening up to him, revealing tiny bits of my childhood in the orphanage and my miserable existence now. I was hoping perhaps he would help me trace my roots and as he walked away I pleaded, "Please don't tell Jean what I told you." If only he knew the real problems, I thought, watching him leave the ward.

That evening I was transferred to the unit and later had a visit from Tommy and Jean. As before, Jean was furious and the look on her face would have soured milk.

She started yelling, "This is a psychiatric ward for mad people!" Nurses and other patients turned to hear the commotion but she didn't care, "What are the neighbours and the people at the factory going to think of you now, knowing you are mad?"

The following morning a very tall man, wearing glasses with one broken lens approached me, "I am one of the psychiatrists in the unit Marie. I will be having a chat with you each day with the hope of us getting to the root of your problems." You could do with a new pair of glasses, I thought, as I stared up at him. "You'll never be able to help me," I muttered under my breath, not caring if he heard me or not, "at least not as long as Tommy and Jean are around." He was smartly dressed with a suit and spoke with a pleasant accent. The nurse informed me about the visiting hours and meal times, finishing by saying, "Marie you will be alright here, we will help you." Sadly, I just wasn't interested in anything she or anybody else said.

Tommy and Jean were the only people to visit me in the unit over the next nine months, other than a brief visit from a priest. Jean's behaviour was the same every time, rambling on at the top of her voice and moaning about her problems at home. When she found out that part of the treatment would be a consultation with a psychiatrist every day, she told me not to open up to him, "Don't be telling that doctor anything." She ranted and raved so much about mental illness that I started to believe I really was going mad. "Once you have a mental illness no one will want to associate with you," she finished. Any hopes of getting better or help were dashed by Jean's attitude. "The psychiatrist can hypnotise you to force you to reveal information about us you know," Jean announced on one visit, so when the psychiatrist suggested hypnosis I bluntly refused. I was more worried about the life I was living than expressing my true feelings and learnt to build a huge wall around myself. Just like the wall that hemmed me in the orphanage for many years, I was trapped by this wall and refused to let the doctors or nurses in. I felt very alone.

Instead of doing something drastic like slashing my wrists, I refused to eat and was physically sick after meals. I think the nurses realised what I was doing, so a decision was made to supervise me at all times, even during my visits to the toilet and shower room.

One day, Jean visited and as usual was quizzing me about the psychiatrist and ranting about having no one to clean the house or walk the dogs when I just snapped. I grabbed hold of her and screamed, "For Christ's sake, get the heck out of my sight and leave me alone! What about asking how the hell I feel?" I completely lost it and with all of my five stone of body weight lashed out at her. I suddenly felt somebody jab me in the bottom and shortly after that I was out cold. It was the following morning before I woke to find the psychiatrist sitting at my bedside. He explained that he had no option but to sedate me to calm me down but he understood my reasons for the outburst.

I didn't have a visit from Jean for the rest of the week and was content with that. As the days and weeks passed Jean only visited once a day so during her absence I was able to talk to the psychiatrist quite freely but still hid well behind the wall I had built around me. I had simply lost all trust in human nature.

I began putting on a little weight but still needed somebody that I could trust to help me make sense of what was happening to my mind. Some weeks later I was introduced to a social worker and she was the first person to suggest that it might be better for me to get my own place on discharge from hospital. Maybe now someone is hearing my cry for help I thought, as I sat in the small room listening to her. "Marie, when you get discharged I will call to the house to see you." "Can you get me a place without me having to go home?" I pleaded. "Well, let's see how things go Marie," she said as she got up to leave the room. As I watched her leave, I had a feeling that this was going to be a lost cause.

A few days later the social worker asked to see Jean and as predicted Jean blew a fuse and refused to speak about anything. I just sat there without the courage to speak. When Jean left the room, the social worker announced that she would do her best. I thought differently! Months later I had gained enough weight to be discharged from the unit but my mental and emotional issues were unresolved.

Unfortunately, I had to go back to stay with Jean and Tommy, the very people who were part of my problems. It was as if I had never been away, apart from now I was paranoid that people were staring at me as I walked up and down the street. I wondered it Jean had told the neighbourhood about my breakdown. I returned to work at the factory and on the first day back Maura asked, "Where have you been Marie?' I just sat down at my sewing machine and answered, "Nowhere."

A few days later I arrived home from work to Jean announcing, "That social worker called twice this week but I soon told her to stay away from here." "When is she coming back?" I asked, thinking maybe the social worker would help me find my way to freedom. "Are you deaf? She's not coming to this house. I told her you were fine," she said adamantly. While listening to her a strange thought entered my mind; maybe it's her who needs psychiatric help, not me!

Another year passed and things weren't any better. Life just consisted of walking the dogs, feeding the cats, cleaning the house, working in the stitching factory and caring for Tommy and Jean. If I didn't have a plan for the future then I was doomed and I wondered was the breakdown a wake up call?

I did a lot of soul searching while working away in the factory and realised that if I was prepared to sit at a sewing machine day in and day out then there was no hope for my future. I knew I needed a next step and it came one evening when I lifted the paper after Tommy and Jean had gone out. I noticed the jobs column and reading though it I saw an advert for orderlies in a local hospital. I took the writing pad from the cabinet and without hesitation wrote away for an application, posting my letter before Tommy and Jean got home. God knows what my writing was like, but at this stage I didn't care. To my amazement, a few days later the form arrived, which I got hold of before Jean saw the post. I filled it in that day and posted it on my way home from work.

Weeks passed with no response, so I was beginning to think that I hadn't been accepted. However, one day, while working at my sewing machine, the strangest feeling came over me. I suddenly switched off the machine, got up from my seat and slowly walked past other workers, who at this stage were staring at me. I walked to the end of the factory where Mr Brown's office was, in full view of the factory floor and knocked on the door. I entered before he had time to respond.

"Mr Brown, can you get somebody else to do my work, I am going to be a nurse," I was frightened by the words coming out of my mouth but continued, "I have been working here for the past four years and now the time has come to move on." He got up from his chair, smiled at me and said, "Marie you do what you feel is right for you, I certainly won't stop you. But you know that your job will be here for you if you decide to come back." My God I thought, this man is actually happy for me, I can't believe he isn't cross! "And the very best of luck in what ever you decide to do Marie," he echoed as I toddled out of his office.

I sauntered to my machine with my head in the air, as though I hadn't a care in the world, collected my coat and strolled toward the door. "Marie, where are you going?" Maura asked. I smiled at her and replied loudly to make sure she and other workers would hear my announcement, "I am out of here for good and going to be a nurse." She, along with other stitchers looked at each other and laughed but I ignored them and walked out of the factory gate and onto the Donegall Road for what I hoped would be my last time.

On my way home my actions began to sink in and I realised I had no idea how to explain the situation to Jean. I was frightened but a voice in my head piped up, "Marie, there is more to life than this miserable existence, grab it while you can." I certainly couldn't change the past but I could change the future, and no matter the effort it took, I was about to do just that!

Chapter Five

THE STRUGGLE TO SUCCEED

BECAUSE I WAS EARLIER than usual, Jean wasn't standing at the garden gate. I felt my heart pounding in anticipation as the dogs greeted me. They always gave me a better welcome then Jean. "Why are you home so early?" she asked as I entered the sitting room. "I've left the factory and won't be back," I declared. "Jesus, did you get the sack?" she demanded. "I'm not going back as I've applied for a job in the hospital," I answered quite calmly. "My God, Tommy, did you hear that? She's left the bloody factory and where the hell do you think we are going to get the money from to pay damn bills?" she roared at me and I wondered how on earth an asthmatic like her could shout all this without a breath."Say what you like but I am not going back," I replied, leaving the room before she could say another word. I could hear her and Tommy arguing as I went upstairs.

Since I wasn't going to the factory anymore, Jean increased my work around the house, finding more and more things that needed done. I continued to cry myself to sleep at night until, in 1972, things changed. I was called for an interview but worried dreadfully that Jean would insist on going with me and make a scene. She was capable of doing anything that would ruin my chances of success. I didn't want anybody knowing my past and on the day of the interview I panicked that she would contact the hospital and reveal all about my nervous breakdown. However, I tried to be positive, as any hint of weakness could be used by Jean as a weapon.

True to form, as I headed out the door, she shouted after me, "They'll ask all about your education, don't you know that?" I thought about what she'd said on route to the interview and practiced the answers I could give if the subject arose.

At the hospital I was escorted into a small room, asked to wait and told that somebody would come for me shortly. I sat for a few minutes alone and began to shake, saying to myself, "Please, please accept me for the post." After a few minutes a lady appeared in the room and said, "Miss Rogers, please follow me." I nervously followed her to another room, which had a large table in the centre with another lady in a very smart navy uniform sat behind it. The lady who escorted me into the room took a seat beside the other lady and asked me to also take a seat.

Both women looked stern but somehow this didn't frighten me in any way. One lady introduced herself as

Miss Strong, the Matron and her colleague as Mrs Johnston, the Assistant Matron. Mrs Johnston was quite small, with very short curly hair, while Miss Strong was tall, with grey shoulder length hair that was tied back and hidden under a neat white cap.

They began to ask me questions and although they came thick and fast, for some unknown reason I felt very relaxed. I was able to answer everything without hesitating or stumbling, even when Mrs Johnston asked, "Are you always so thin Miss Rogers?" To my own surprise I answered without even a thought, "Oh I've had a terrible flu with a tummy bug and still getting over it." Thankfully they seemed to believe me. Throughout the interview I felt like someone or something was guiding me but perhaps I was just prepared for all eventualities.

"All new staff must have a medical before working at this hospital," Mrs Johnston announced. "That's no problem," I answered quietly, hoping the medical wasn't because of my thinness. "Does that mean I have the job?" I asked. "We will let you know in a few days time by letter Miss Rogers," Miss Strong replied and at that thanked me for attending. I had a feeling that I would be accepted for the position and almost tumbled out of the room in my excitement. It had been such a huge decision to apply for the job in the hospital and now that I had completed my first big interview, the feeling was just brilliant.

I didn't expect any encouragement when I returned home and although Jean asked, "Well how did it go?"

There was little enthusiasm in her voice. "Did they ask what school you came from and about your family?" I knew she was referring to the orphanage and the special school, but I just ignored her and left the room. After living with her for almost five years, I could read her like a book, and knew she was trying to provoke me.

When a week had passed without word of whether I had been accepted for the post, Jean started to moan about money and bills. However, a reply finally did arrive a few weeks later. Thankfully I got to the letterbox before Jean and almost ripped the envelope in my hurry to open it. My hands were shaking as read the words "Pleased to inform you". That was all I needed to see. I shouted from my bedroom, "Oh my God! I got the job." Making sure Jean could hear the excitement in my voice, I added, "I've done it and all on my own."

The whole way to the hospital for my medical I asked myself, "What will I say if they ask about my medical history?" Thankfully, I needn't have worried, as I passed with flying colours. This was the start of a new chapter in my life and I felt that the decision to leave the factory was the right one. When I received the letter telling me that I had been successful and was to report to Miss Strong's office on a particular date in 1972, I couldn't explain the excitement that I was experiencing, it was so overwhelming. I lay awake for hours the night before I started, thinking of my impending employment but still had my usual tears before going to sleep.

My first day at Belvoir Park Hospital was such a memorable day. On arriving at Miss Strong's office, she sent for Mrs Johnston who took me to the sewing room to be fitted with a uniform. It was a green dress and a white cap with green trimming around the edge. I felt so proud standing in front of the mirror looking at this smartly dressed new member of the hospital staff.

I think Mrs Johnston liked me. She took me to ward 4b and introduced to Sister Sweeney, who was in charge. Mrs Johnston then left and Sister Sweeney explained the duties of a ward orderly. She was a lady in her 40s and quite serious looking but somehow I was quite comfortable with her. She was very strict but also extremely fair and ran the ward military style. She was held in high regard by all her staff from the most senior nurse to the domestics.

The list of my duties was endless but hard work was never a problem to me, I was more worried about carrying out my duties to her satisfaction. When she explained that she expected things done well and that I would receive a report every so often, this made me even more determined to give my all and not let her down. However, I needn't have worried. I seemed to carry out my duties to Sister Sweeney's expectations and received excellent reports from her.

I loved my new job and was so happy seeing firsthand the work carried out by the medical profession that I was so proud to be a part of. I enjoyed it so much that I never wanted to leave the hospital, especially knowing

I had further work to do at home, where no thanks was given. Days turned into weeks and weeks into months, and I really couldn't have been more happily employed. I sometimes looked at the work that the nurses were doing and thought perhaps I could do this too one day. However, I knew my education would prove a stumbling block in any career progression.

One day the Senior Nurse said that Sister Sweeney wanted to see me in her office. On arrival, Sister Sweeny informed me, "Miss Rogers, Miss Strong would like to see you in her office at 11.00 am." My heart missed a beat, because when staff were asked to the Matron's office, it often meant they were in trouble.

At 11.00 am I headed to Miss Strong's office and before knocking on the door, checked that my uniform was neat and tidy and that my hair was well tied back under my cap. I was pleasantly surprised when Miss Strong said, "Miss Rogers I have your first report in front of me and see that Sister Sweeney is very impressed with your standard of work. I have spoken to the nursing tutor about you and we both feel that you should apply for the entrance exam for nurse training." I must be hearing things, I thought, looking between her and a man sitting beside her. "This is Mr Bryan," she explained, as the man stood up to shake my hand. He echoed Miss Strong's words, "I strongly think that you should consider doing the entrance exam." Miss Strong continued, "I am so impressed with Sister Sweeney's report that I am offering you a nursing auxiliary position as and from next week. I have informed the sewing room so go tomorrow and collect your new uniform." I was both shocked by her announcement but also extremely excited. I stood high that day thinking that these three people recognised that I had the capability of becoming a nursing auxiliary and maybe even a nurse. The feeling was just incredible.

The following day I walked into ward 4b proudly dressed in my new uniform. Again Sister Sweeney explained my duties, which were more hands on but still included plenty of cleaning. She also said that she would expect more from me but I was more willing and determined than ever.

I was going to be working more closely with the nurses and as I followed them to the ward, Sister Sweeney announced, "Report to my office first thing tomorrow morning, I will supervise you bathing a baby to see how you get on Miss Rogers." As an orderly, the only contact with the babies was to collect their soiled nappies from the cubicle, clean the room, replace clean nappies and remove used baby bottles. Now I was going to actually touch them and I couldn't sleep that night with the excitement of it all.

The next morning, Sister Sweeney escorted me to the cubicle nearest her office so that I would be in full view of her. There, in a small cot, was the tiniest baby smiling up at us. Sister had a trolley with all the necessary items required and explained the procedure of bathing a baby. I listened intently but nervously, scared that I would slip up and let myself down. "Now I want you to bathe the baby. Come here and lift the child out of the cot," she said confidently. "Goodness sister!" I whispered following her instructions, "He is slipping out of my hand Sister." But she soon reassured me with her confident manner and before long the nervousness left me. I was bathing the baby as if I had done it dozens of times, listening carefully to her instructions as I did so. When finished, I placed the tiny infant back in the cot and noticed Sister Sweeney was grinning at me from her office. "That is the best and most enjoyable thing I have ever done sister," I gushed as she came out of her office. She must have thought I was mad! I learnt so much from Sister Sweeney and her staff during my time working with them.

After about two years of working on the ward, I was summoned once again to Miss Strong's office. Knowing that I wasn't in any trouble this time, I wondered what she wanted me for. On entering, I saw Mr Bryan sitting beside her again. He was quite a small man with receding hair, an air of confidence and a serious expression. He was a senior lecturer, so I often saw him coming in and out of the ward to speak to the nurses but I hadn't had any direct dealings with him. Going by the nurses, however, he seemed to be highly respected throughout the hospital.

It was Mr Bryan who spoke this time, "Miss Strong and I have been discussing your ward reports from Sister Sweeney that are still quite good. Your eagerness to learn has not been unnoticed. Miss Strong and I would like you to apply for the State Enrolment Nursing at this hospital. The exam would be at the hospital in a few weeks time."

My heart missed a beat and I simply stared at them, not believing what I was hearing. Where they actually asking me to sit an exam to become a nurse? After the initial shock, I blabbered, "Mr Bryan, I have never done exams." "Oh don't worry about that Miss Rogers I am sure you'll do very well," he said reassuringly, "you'll receive a letter regarding the date of the exam and will be allowed to leave the ward to do it."

He explained briefly about the course and it all sounded so grand and tempting. However, the thought of sitting an exam that would decide whether I nursed or not terrified me. I wanted to shout, "You don't know how stupid I really am!" Miss Strong interrupted my thoughts by saying, "You can go back on duty now." A long glass corridor separated the various wards and I ran up the corridor like a five year old, excitedly wanting to tell Sister Sweeney and the staff what I had just been offered.

"You will get the exam," Ann, the Senior Nurse of the ward said while other nurses echoed her remark. Ann was in the ward when I started and we got on very well. I wished that I felt as confident as she did but with my lack of education I didn't think I had a hope of passing this exam or any other exam for that matter. All the same, I quizzed Ann about the exam, which she had done many years earlier, and when I heard that it consisted of Maths and English I was even more frightened.

Jean's response to my good news was as negative as ever, "Sure you're not educated or capable of doing exams for nursing." I didn't need her to remind me about that but in some ways I felt she was probably right. I could see myself standing in a nurse's uniform, but getting there was going to be the biggest challenge of my life.

I received the date for the exam a few days later and arrangements were made for me to get off duty to sit the exam in the School of Nursing at the hospital. On the morning of the exam I spent more time in the toilet than out on the ward! I headed over to the school at 1.30 pm and on entering the waiting area, noticed about 40 other people. The girls waiting were young school leavers, which made me feel old as I was in my mid-20s. We were all ushered into a large hall, with rows of small tables and chairs. My heart starting thumping when I saw the exam sheets on the tables as we made our way to seats. Once we were all seated, it was so quiet that you could've heard a pin drop. After a brief moment Mr Bryan explained the layout of the exam and how long we had to complete it. He wished us luck and told us to start.

As I looked at the exam sheet, I could barely remember my own name, never mind read the questions. Breaking out in a sweat, I realised I was staring at English and Maths questions and hadn't a clue were to begin! I glanced around the room at the other girls writing like mad and with nothing yet written on my paper, I started shaking so much that I struggled to hold the pen. My mouth became so dry that my lips were nearly sticking together and after a few minutes I raised my hand for Mr Bryan's attention. Other people looked over at me, as Mr Bryan approached. "Could I please have a glass of water?" I asked with a husky voice. When he brought the water back he said in a whisper, "Do your best Miss Rogers." I looked down at the paper again but after a few seconds I realised if I didn't do something I was going to have a panic attack. I got up from my chair, walked up to Mr Bryan, handed my paper to him and quietly left the room.

I headed straight to the toilet and blurted out aloud, "The damn nuns are to blame for this." Any hope of becoming a nurse had been shattered because they deprived me of a good education. As I was coming out of the toilet I bumped into Mr Bryan who knew that I looked very upset. "Don't worry, you did your best," he said very quietly. I just wanted to get away from him and everybody else. I felt so ashamed.

Three weeks later I received a phone call at home asking me to report to Miss Strong the following day before going on duty. It didn't take a genius to work out what Miss Strong was going to say. "You have failed the exam Miss Rogers," she said calmly. I sat staring at her, wanting to cry with the shame of failing but thankfully I didn't. "I knew it Miss Strong," I confessed, "I have never done exams." I was careful not to mention the special school. "I think you should go to evening classes and if you can gain the necessary O Levels required for nursing without the entrance exam then you should consider going down that route," she advised. This was good and bad news for me, as I was going to have to achieve at least five O Levels!

I thought long and hard about what Miss Strong had suggested but it just seemed impossible to study for O Levels while working and living with Tommy and Jean. Some months later, however, I decided that I had to try and started attending evening classes. Getting to the evening classes proved quite difficult combined with all the travelling to work, so I decided to apply for a post closer to home at Belfast City Hospital and was accepted. I needed money to pay for the evening classes, which of course became an issue with Jean. She still had control over my wages and didn't want to admit that it was my money that I wanted to use to pay for the classes. However, I persisted and eventually she gave in.

The time had come for me to move on and in 1975 I worked my last shift in Belvoir Park Hospital. Sister Sweeney had a lovely tea party for me and presented me with a little dictionary. "I hope this dictionary helps you with your studies Miss Rogers," she said, as we gathered round the table that was spread with tea and buns. Those were the days when the ward Sister didn't call you by your name. Everything was very formal.

I was sad to leave Belvoir and have many fond memories of the three years I worked in ward 4b. I made many friends there but sadly could never invite them to Jean's house after I left. I will never forget Sister

Sweeney's encouragement and hold her in high regard to this day.

I started working in the Belfast City Hospital as a nursing auxiliary in a male cardiac ward. The work was very different from working with babies but I settled in well. Sister Neill, the ward Sister, was a tall woman with very sharp features. She was just as strict as Sister Sweeney and also ran the ward military style. Thankfully I got on very well with her.

The ward overlooked the Erskine House, which contained the nurses's home, and three times a year groups of 50 to 100 young people arrived to begin a nursing career. Every time there was an intake of new recruits, I watched them arrive with their parents and wished so much that I was joining them. By this stage I hadn't long started studying English Language and Human Biology O Levels. Sister Neill was a great help to me with my Biology but I found the studying very difficult and seemed to fail one exam after another. Jean of course didn't help matters. I often missed classes because she needed something done, there was a problem with the animals, Tommy wasn't well or she was admitted to hospital.

One Christmas the staff arranged to go to a dance and after much arguing Jean allowed me to go. She still managed to control the situation by only giving me the money to get into the dance and bus fare home. On arriving home around 1.00 am I was shocked to see a furious Jean standing in the hall waiting for me. She ranted and raved so much that I never went to another dance. She won again!

Every Monday I played badminton at a club within the hospital, much to Jean's disgust. I was trying to become more assertive and determined in the things that I wanted to do. I really enjoyed the badminton, entering as many competitions as possible and I even started winning trophies. Attending my evening classes and playing badminton provided a great escape for me. However, there was always something for me to do when I arrived home, even at 11.00 pm, such as cleaning or walking the dogs.

I was also now caring for Tommy, as he was in the early stages of dementia. As Jean became more obese I ended up looking after her very personal care too, which I knew she was quite capable of doing herself. One morning I left the basin of water beside her, saying, "You give yourself a wash while I light the fire and get the cats sorted out." Instead of agreeing she went crazy. Snapping the cloth from my hand she yelled at the top of her voice, "Christ almighty! You don't give a damn about us; next you'll be shoving us into a nursing home." She had a shrewd way of throwing the guilt back at me and as usual I gave into her tantrums.

Four years had passed when I heard that the national entrance exam for nursing could be sat again. I decided to apply to re-sit it but unfortunately failed the exam again. At least this time I could actually see the questions and didn't sweat or feel as nervous as before. I decided not to let the failure deter me and continued with my classes. Miss Strong was the one who recognised that I had something to give and encouraged me to study, and I wasn't going to let her down. I resat the exam for the fourth time and contacted the School of Nursing to find out the result of my last attempt. To my amazement, I was told that I was on the border line of passing and was advised to re-sit the exam as soon as possible. To be so near yet so far from gaining a place in nurse training was incredible. My confidence was building and on the fifth attempt I somehow felt like 'this is it' but didn't want to get too optimistic. I sat the exam early in 1979 and was actually able to answer most of the questions.

In November of 1979 I received a reply from the examining board. I expected to see the now familiar words jump out at me, 'Sorry but', however, to my sheer delight I was reading that I was to attend an interview for State Enrolment Nursing. "My God I've done it!" I screamed, running up and down the stairs. My hand was shaking as I read aloud the contents of the letter, making sure Tommy and Jean heard every word. Surprisingly, Jean actually seemed pleased for me but of course she had to have the last word, "You won't be able to go to the badminton any more because you will have to stay in and study. You'll find it hard because those wee girls will be more educated than you." I was so overjoyed that the hard work had finally paid off that I didn't care what she said. My career in nursing was about to begin and nothing else mattered. Life was going to change.

I couldn't wait to get on duty that afternoon to tell Sister Neill my fantastic news. She had been such a great help and on the occasions I had failed exams she always encouraged me to keep at it. "Yes I know you passed," she said, "I was contacted by one of the tutors this morning; I am so pleased for you Marie." I spent the rest of the day in a dream like state, thinking that very soon I was going to join the ranks of the nursing professionals.

A few days before my interview Sister Neill explained some interview techniques. By the time I went for the interview I was excited but also nervous. It was up to me to impress the panel enough to accept me for the next intake. Lots of people had passed the exam but failed the interview and their medical, and I certainly didn't want to join them.

There were three people on the interviewing panel and one of them was Mrs Logan, Head of Nursing Education, who was feared by all. She introduced the rest of the panel before asking me what interests I had. To my surprise she added, "You should be very proud of yourself Miss Rogers; your marks were high enough to do the three year Registered Nursing." I had a smile from ear to ear. "However I think you should do the State Enrolment Course first and perhaps later do your Registration. I notice you live quite close therefore you won't need accommodation," she continued. My smile faded slightly.

I wanted so much to ask for accommodation but I was scared she would ask why so I just answered, "That's fine." Looking from one person to the other on the panel, I sensed they were happy with my interview. Mrs Logan informed me of the impending course and the date for my medical, before finishing, "If your medical goes well you will start State Enrolment Nurse Training in January 1980." The interview lasted about 30 minutes and once out of the building I ran as fast as I could to the ward to inform Sister Neill of my good news. My excitement was overwhelming and I wanted to tell every person I met that I was going to be a nurse.

Arriving home that evening I announced my good news to Tommy and Jean. "Did they ask about your education? Don't build your hopes up because they'll likely take younger girls first," Jean replied sharply. I ignored her comments and got stuck into cleaning the place. I then took the dogs for a walk to get some time on my own to reflect on the day.

In December 1979 I received the official letter giving the start date for my training in January 1980. The day I left the cardiac ward was an emotional but happy one. Sister Neill, the nurses and medical staff on the ward organised a party for me. They presented me with a beautiful little Tyrone Crystal basket, which took pride of place in the parlour cabinet. I may have known them for only five years but they had be so supportive throughout my time with them.

Lisieux Private Nursing Home, where I was born in February 1950. It was situated opposite the Benn Hospital at 69 Clifton Street, near Carlisle Circus, Belfast. (© *National Museums Northern Ireland, Collection Ulster Folk & Transport Museum, HOYFM.WAG.3693*)

A photograph from an outing to Ballyhoran, Co Down, in 1956/7. I am quite young here, about 6 or 7 years old, and just visible second from the left.

This one was taken at the seaside when I was 9 or 10. I have no memory of ever having my picture taken but the nuns would often say "Stand there" and we would do as we were told. I am in the front row, fourth from the left.

Another group photograph, possibly taken at Glenariff, Co Antrim around 1960. Again I am about 10 years old. I am kneeling in the third row, just left of centre.

A front view of Nazareth House and the nuns's gardens. The actual entrance was at a gated hut in the wall to the left. The building in the background, emerging to the right, housed both St Ann's and the senior girls's dormitories.

Myself at the entrance to the Special School I attended in Whiteabbey. It was demolished in the 1990s.

The glass front of the unit for the Care of the Elderly (ladies). The sloping roof to the left was the Chapel within the orphanage.

The Holy Rosary Chapel. Behind it was the orchard that we pinched apples and pears from. The red brick building on the right housed Our Lady's and Sacred Heart's dormitories, and a hall on the ground floor. In front of this was the playground.

A photograph
of me at 19,
taken in my
friend's garden
in 1969.

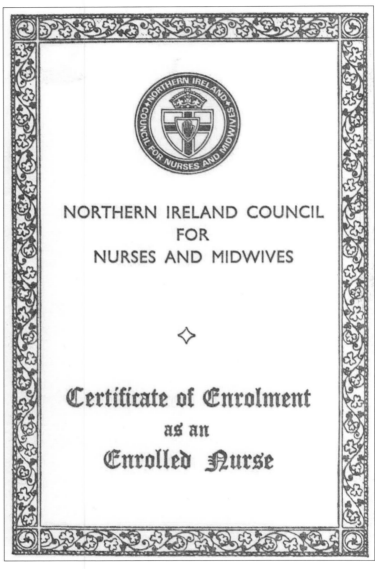

NORTHERN IRELAND COUNCIL
FOR
NURSES AND MIDWIVES

◇

Certificate of Enrolment
as an
Enrolled Nurse

My State Enrolment Nursing Certificate, which I achieved in 1981.

Enrolment No.....7143.........

NORTHERN IRELAND COUNCIL FOR NURSES AND MIDWIVES
(1970 Ch. II)

It is hereby Certified that

..........MARIE THERESE ROGERS..............

was admitted to the Roll of Nurses maintained by the Northern Ireland Council for Nurses and Midwives,

on ....7th October 1981.............................

and that...she.....is entitled, in pursuance of the Nurses and Midwives Act (Northern Ireland), 1970, to take and use the title of "Enrolled Nurse."

Chairman of Council

The Seal of the Council was hereunto affixed this

.Twenty-sixth.....day of

......October...........19 81.

Director of Nursing and Midwifery Education

A portrait taken in 1982, a year after I qualified as a nurse. I am 32.

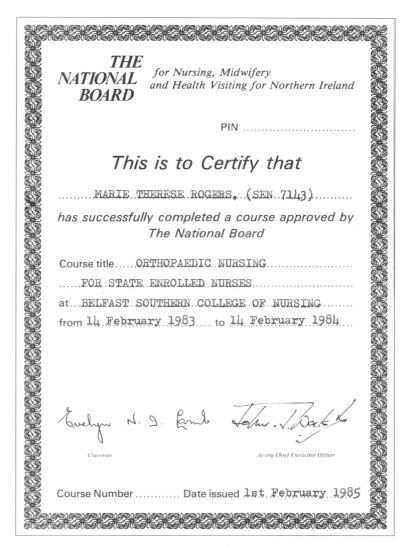

THE
NATIONAL
BOARD

for Nursing, Midwifery and Health Visiting for Northern Ireland

PIN ....

This is to Certify that

.... MARIE THERESE ROGERS, (SEN 7143) ....

has successfully completed a course approved by The National Board

Course title..... ORTHOPAEDIC NURSING.....................

...... FOR STATE ENROLLED NURSES.........................

at ... BELFAST SOUTHERN COLLEGE OF NURSING ....

from 14 February 1983 .... to 14 February 1984 ...

Evelyn N. I. Lamb

Chairman

John J. Back

Acting Chief Executive Officer

Course Number .... Date issued 1st February 1985

My certificate for my Diploma of Orthopaedic Nursing, which I achieved in 1985.

Some of the nursing staff in the Cardiac Ward of Belfast City Hospital in 1976. I am sitting in the middle, wearing my nursing auxiliary uniform.

A photograph taken of me at my friend Patricia's home around 1989. I am 39.

MARIE TERESE ROGERS.

BORN 26 FEBRUARY 1950
     AT, 65, CLIFTON ST.
BAPTIZED : ST. PATRICKS.

MOTHER JOSEPHINE ROGERS

OF: BAYVIEW HOTEL. MAIN ST.
    KILLYBEGS CO. DONEGAL

NOTE:
   N.H. THIS CHILD FOR ADOPTION
   PLACED FOR ADOPTION WITH
   MRS ████████ ANNSBRO' CO DOWN.

A piece of paper given to me by one of the Sisters of Nazareth in the 1990s.

The Nazareth Orphanage was finally demolished in 2001 to make way for a new development of apartments.

The work beginning outside Our Lady's and the Sacred Heart's dormitories.

A front view of Nazareth House being demolished. To the right is St Ann's dormitory wing.

A photograph of me visiting the site of the demolition. I am holding an early draft of this book.

Mixed emotions as Nazareth House falls

Orphan's story rises from the rubble

Marie Therese Rogers surveys the ruins of Nazareth House

The famous Nazareth House orphanage on the Ormeau Road was home to thousands of orphaned and abandoned children over the years.

But as the bulldozers moved in this week to demolish the 125-year-old building, one woman who will remember the children's home long after the site is flattened is Marie Therese Rogers.

Sent to Nazareth House when she was just four days old, Marie Therese – who now lives on the Lisburn Road – has written a moving book about her life as an orphan there.

"The only home I had ever known was Nazareth House. I lived there for 17 years," said Marie Therese.

"When it came to putting that life onto paper it was very traumatic, but it was also therapy for me."

Writing about the time that she spent in the home may have been a struggle for Marie, but her new fight is trying to find a publisher

for the book that lifts the lid on Nazareth House.

"I seem to have found myself in a Catch-22 situation. I have been told that for a publisher to take your book you have to be well known writer. But I haven't had the chance to get well known. I think that this book will be of interest to lots of people, not just those raised in children's homes."

As the walls come down on the famous orphanage, Marie says that she has mixed feelings about the demise of the institution where she spent her entire childhood.

"On one hand I am sad to see it go, but on the other hand I'm glad that children are no longer being brought up in such a cold and impersonal way.

"To be in a children's home is like being a number – you are no longer a person or a child, you are just a statistic."

> "In a children's home you aren't a person, just a statistic"

The fight to have her book published has lead Marie to many places – including an appearance on Esther Ransen's talk show.

"I hope that by making these appeals that someone will advise me on the best way to have the book put into print.

"It was an extremely emotional experience writing this book, and I think that will comes across to the reader," she added.

"I wrote the book about orphanage life through a child's eyes and then followed the search

for my natural parents, and ultimately how I came to find them."

Marie is also appealing for anyone who spent time in the home to get in touch for a weekend reunion that has been planned for later this year.

"It is appropriate that in the year that the home has been demolished that we all come together and discuss our experiences.

"None of us forgot when we walked out the doors of Nazareth House – the memories, good and bad, stay with you for the rest of your life."

Marie Therese can be contacted for details about her book, or the Nazareth Lodge reunion, on 028 9087 2665.

A newspaper article, with me holding an early draft of this book.

My first cousin Denis (Dinnie) Moloney and I at his home near Cloughjordan, Tipperary, in 2009.

IHS

IN LOVING MEMORY OF
DENIS MOLONEY
FHILL,
DIED 23rd AUG. 1913,
AND HIS WIFE NORA
DIED 8th JAN. 1931
THEIR SON PATRICK
DIED 6th JUNE 1971
THEIR SON DENIS
DIED 16th JAN. 1981

R. I. P.
ERECTED BY THEIR FAMILY

Dinnie took me to my father's grave in September 2009.

A photograph taken at my 60th birthday party of three of my first cousins (l-r) Nora, Martina and Dinnie, and myself in the front row.

At home reflecting during the Historical Abuse Inquiry in 2014. *(Courtesy Daily Mirror. Picture by Justin Kernoghan)*

At the end of my duty, before leaving the ward for the last time, the staff, including Sister Neill, grabbed hold of me. They carried me to the bathroom and dunked me into a bath of lukewarm water, poured talcum powder all over me and then scattered like doves let lose from a cage. This treatment was meted out to staff when they left wards in which they had worked for any length of time. The day before I called to tell the Nursing Officer my good news. "I can only wish you every success at the nursing and you know that you would be very welcome back on any of my wards when you qualify Miss Rogers," she said kindly. She received reports every six months and informed me that my reports were always very good.

After watching so many new recruits enter Erskine House over the past five years, I was finally going to join them. Walking into the building that Monday morning to begin my nursing career was my proudest moment. I glanced up at the window of the ward expecting to see somebody watching me but there was nobody there.

I stood among a large group of students in a huge hall. Standing on the stage was none other than Mrs Logan, who gave us a lecture on what would be expected from us during our time in the nursing profession. As I listened, I looked around the room at the people with me and noticed only a few of my age group, as most were younger. I wondered did any of them have the same difficulties that I had before getting to this point. My thoughts were interrupted on hearing Mrs Logan say,

"Now ladies, should any of you fail an exam twice during your training, you will be asked to discontinue and leave the hospital." My mind swirled as I realised that the hard work wasn't over yet but I reminded myself that I was here and that's what mattered.

As we all strolled out of the hall, along with family members who had accompanied their sons and daughters, I felt quite awkward being alone. Before leaving the house that morning, Jean had insisted on going with me but I wasn't having any of it. I told her that nobody was allowed to accompany the new students, which was a white lie on my part!

The following 18 months were absolutely brilliant and I enjoyed every second. My training took place between Belfast City Hospital, Musgrave Park Hospital and Lagan Valley Hospital in Lisburn. There were exams every four weeks and thankfully I coped quite well. Although I continued caring for Tommy, the house and the animals during my training, I didn't fail any of the exams.

In 1981, I sat my final exam, knowing it was crucial that I passed. There was a lot of trouble in Belfast that day, with bomb scares all over the city. Quite a few of the girls arrived late and one poor girl was refused entry to the examination hall as we were already doing the exam. We heard later that she sat her exam six months later. I wasn't a great one for praying but on this occasion I prayed so hard that I would be able to cope with the examination paper. Amazingly I was able to answer all questions quite well and even had time to check over the paper before it was collected. I came out of the room happy and full of confidence but the exam didn't seem to have gone so well for some of the other girls and there were a few tears shed.

I couldn't believe how quickly the 18 months of training had gone in but the six weeks waiting to hear if I had passed or failed the most important exam of my life felt like forever. In the meantime I had to find a position in the medical, surgical or theatre departments within the three hospitals I had completed my training in. I was fortunate enough to get a position in orthopaedic theatres and told I could stay until my results. I gained great experience there and decided if successful with my finals, I would apply to do the theatre course or the Diploma in Orthopaedic Nursing for Enrolled Nurses.

There was little encouragement from Jean when I told her what my intentions were. "What are you going to do if you don't pass your final exam?" she asked. "I will just have to wait and see, won't I?" I replied. The idea of failing the exam didn't bear thinking about.

Finally, the big day of the results arrived. Every time I answered the telephone in Sister's office my heart sunk, thinking it was Mrs Dougan, our senior tutor, to tell me if I had passed or failed. On first meeting Mrs Dougan I thought she looked very serious but she was actually quite the opposite. Highly regarded by all, it was she who informed the students if they had passed or failed their exams throughout the course. By late afternoon I hadn't heard anything and started to think that I had failed. Nurses who were in my same group rang with their good news and still I hadn't heard anything. One girl also told me that at least six people had failed and this made me feel worse.

Sister Donnelly, the theatre sister called me to her office about 4.00 pm. She was very small and thin, with severe features. She was well respected by the surgeons but could be very sharp with the nursing staff and certainly wasn't as keen to teach as Sister Neill was. As I walked to her office my heart was pounding and I kept saying to myself, "Please, please let me pass!" She was alone in the office and when I entered she handed me the phone without uttering a word. "My God, I have failed haven't I?" I asked.

"Is that Nurse Rogers?" I heard Mrs Dougan's voice say and after a brief moment I answered, "Yes Mrs Dougan, Nurse Rogers speaking, I've failed haven't I?" I pulled a chair over and sat on it waiting for her response. For a few seconds there was complete silence before she announced briskly, "Nurse Rogers, you are now a State Enrolled Nurse, congratulations!" My head was buzzing as I heard her now distant voice say, "Go out and celebrate your success, you have worked hard for this exam." "Oh my God Mrs Dougan did you say I have passed my finals?" I asked again. "You certainly have," she replied. When I handed the phone back to Sister Donnelly, tears came streaming down my face. "Go on home Nurse Rogers,

I am pleased and happy for you," she said as I left her office.

With a spring in my step I literally ran the whole way up the Lisburn Road eager to let Tommy and Jean know that I had done it. I had achieved my goal in becoming a qualified nurse. I think Jean was actually pleased for me but didn't openly say so. I didn't care now; I was officially a qualified nurse and that was all that mattered to me.

I continued to work in orthopaedic theatres for a few more weeks before getting my first post as a qualified State Enrolled Nurse in a children's orthopaedic ward at Musgrave Park Hospital. I loved it. I was overwhelmed the day I received my State Enrolled Certificate showing I was a qualified nurse. That was the final proof of my achievement and goodness me, I was one happy woman.

In early 1983 I heard about a Diploma in Orthopaedic Nursing for State Enrolled Nurses. I applied and was accepted. The course started on St Valentine's Day and four friends from my enrolment course started with me. We were told to count ourselves lucky as over 200 nurses had applied for the course and only six were accepted. I was determined to do well in this course as my ultimate aim was to do my State Registered Nursing. I found the Diploma was much harder than the enrolment course but thankfully I coped with it.

During the course we were sent to various departments within the orthopaedic hospital. One day, while in theatres, we were receiving a lecture from the theatre sister in a very small room that looked more like a storeroom than a lecture room with no windows. At first I was listening intently but after some minutes, I must have dozed off. I was exhausted at times with all that was going on at Jean's house. I woke up to silence and everybody in the room looking at me, including the theatre sister. "My goodness, it's very warm in here, isn't it?" I asked, as one of my colleagues laughed but the theatre sister was furious. "Nurse, perhaps you could tell us what is so funny?" she asked before glaring at me, "It would be a good idea if you could manage a few early nights nurse Rogers, then maybe you might stay awake long enough to listen to a lecture."

Like my Enrolment Nursing, there were plenty of exams but thankfully I passed them all, and in 1984 all six of us passed the Orthopaedic Diploma. Another certificate arrived a few weeks later and I felt that my dreams were now becoming a reality. I had a flash back to the day in the factory that I turned my machine off, walked into Mr Brown's office and told him I was going to be a nurse. If he could see me now! However, that chapter of my life was now gone and I was ready for a new one.

Chapter Six

THE TORTURE CONTINUES

WHILE I WAS STUDYING for the Diploma, doing all the cleaning and caring for Tommy, Jean got me a job moonlighting in a nursing home at night. She said that the bills were mounting and the fact that I wasn't cleaning the offices anymore didn't help her financially. She bought a lot of stuff from catalogues, which she didn't always pay for, so this may have been part of it. She also enjoyed betting on the horses. Every day without fail she collected the daily paper, studied the form of the horses, the prices and the jockeys of every race for that day before going to put her bet on. She actually won quite a bit of money but I was living with a compulsive gambler.

Each month Jean arrived up at the ward to collect my pay, much as she had done every Thursday at the factory. The whole situation was so embarrassing and I hadn't the nerve to object to what she was doing.

The moonlighting, combined with extra chores at home was affecting my ability to concentrate on my nursing duties. I was even falling asleep during the ward reports, which got me in trouble many times. Despite my achievements I was still trapped and cried myself to sleep each night wishing for an escape. I was doing so much to satisfy Jean and even my days off were spent cleaning and looking after the animals.

Over time things just seemed to get worse and worse between the two of us. Every Monday, Wednesday and Friday at 3.30 am I was now expected to wash Jean, light the fire, clean the cats's litter trays and make breakfast before she was collected by a friend, who took her to Mass. Using the excuse that she was too breathless and couldn't manage to wash herself, she expected me to do all her personal care.

"Why don't you come to Mass with me?" she asked one morning and I reluctantly went, simply too tired to object and fed up with her going into a temper. So now I was getting up at 3.30 am, going to church at 5.00 am and to work at 8.00 am – it was crazy!

When I went to mass with Jean, I often fell asleep in the church from sheer exhaustion. On one occasion Jean nagged me so much about not going to confession that I went just to shut her up. Anyway, no sooner had I entered the darkness of the confessional than I dozed over. Suddenly the door was opened by a very irate Jean, who made her disgust known by shouting in the quiet church, "Imagine sleeping in the confessional box!" I didn't bother to say anything; I just got up and walked past her. But on the way home she kept on and on, announcing in front of her friend, "Would you believe it, Marie fell asleep in the confessional box?" To my surprise her friend answered, "Sure didn't St Therese fall asleep many times saying her prayers. Did you not know that Jean?" I sat in the back seat grinning, thinking I got one over on you Jean.

I never understood how Jean could sit with her prayer book in the house and attend so many Masses yet at the same time treat me with such contempt. With so much religion pumped into me as a child in the orphanage and now with Jean, God knows by this stage I had had my fill of it.

In 1987 some of my friends from the hospital had decided to go on a pilgrimage to Knock and I went with them. It wasn't the praying that interested me, it was getting away from Jean. It turned out to be an enjoyable day and arriving home very late that evening there she was once again waiting at the gate. Another row ensued because one of the cats had got out onto the main road and was killed. The blame was laid on my shoulders as usual.

Over the years Tommy and Jean managed to accumulate all the stray animals of the day, ending up with eight cats and two dogs. They took little part in caring for them, so any love and attention they got came from me. Strangely enough I felt the animals were a bit like little orphans, trapped like me in this house.

One year I joined the nurse's netball team and while playing one evening I fell and badly tore the ligaments in my ankle. Some of the girls took me to the hospital, where I had my ankle strapped and was told not to put much weight on it. My friends took me home and to my embarrassment Jean simply glared at me and demanded, "Where have you been?" "I have damaged my bloody ankle; thanks for your sympathy," I snapped back. When the girls left she huffed for a while before asking, "What about the decorating?" I yelled at her, "For Christ's sake don't fret, the damn decorating will be done." "Well I hope so because Tommy isn't fit to do it anymore." When Jean wanted anything done Tommy was used as the excuse, just like her asthma.

My ankle didn't improve with the splint, so I also had to have a plaster cast on for nine weeks. During that time I cleaned the house as usual and decorated it to simply avoid further arguments. In spite of my constant cleaning, the house was coming down with horrible cockroaches. If you needed to go to the bathroom during the night, which was downstairs beyond the kitchen, as soon as the light was lit, there they were in their hundreds, running in all directions to escape into the various holes in the floor.

Scarcely a night when by without my sleep being disturbed by Jean having an asthma attack or wanting a wee cup of tea. She would shout from her bedroom, "Marie, I need the oxygen." I would carry the huge oxygen cylinder up the stairs and down again when she had finished with it. "Are you making a wee cup of tea Marie?" she would then ask, pretending to be nice. How could you refuse! Tommy completely ignored her and slept through the whole thing. I found it very sad that a husband would ignore his wife's plea for help but maybe he just wasn't giving in to her like I did.

Tommy's health eventually deteriorated and he became quite difficult to manage. There were days when he just sat staring into the fire and wouldn't even wash or dress himself. I was the one who encouraged him to get washed and take his tablets, and for some reason he often listened to me. With his dementia I think he got to the stage were he didn't know who his wife was any more.

With Tommy's illness he was no longer able to drive so Jean paid for driving lessons for me, of course out of my own wages. In 1977 I passed my driving test and added the role of chauffeur to my list of jobs for Tommy and Jean. On the last Friday of every month, Jean was waiting for me at the gate after work, coat ready, to be taken to the local shop, where boxes were filled to the brim with messages and paid for from my earnings.

Once the messages were organised I had to drive to the other side of Belfast, where an closed order of nuns lived and the boxes were left in a porch for them. However, leaving the messages wasn't good enough for Jean; she insisted on letting the nuns know what she had done for them. Then it was off to the bookies so Jean could put a bet on the horses and collect her winnings, and on to Sandy Row to a tiny corner shop where she collected her weekly intake of snuff. She had told me that snuff was good for her asthma when I caught her inhaling something brown in the sitting room one day. It explained what she had been hiding away in her handkerchief for all those years.

As Jean got older, her behaviour became even stranger. She had never respected my personal space but seemed to get worse the longer I lived with her. One day I was sitting watching the television, a rarity for me, when Jean came into the sitting room. She bent over the chair to hug me and tried to kiss me on the lips. She wasn't usually affectionate, so this took me by surprise. "Jesus Christ, what are you doing?" I shouted, jumping up. "Och stop shouting. I am only fooling around," she yelled back before leaving the room. She also began opening the bathroom door without knocking when I was washing myself. When I protested, she would simply say, "Sure we're all the same." It really gave me the creeps, so I pushed the oil heater against the door to prevent anybody entering after that.

It was so frustrating. I was a qualified nurse, who took charge of ward full of patients, yet I couldn't prevent this woman from controlling me. I did a lot of soul searching and knew in my heart that things had to change. Now that I had made this decision, the questions were how and when?

Chapter Seven

FREEDOM AT LAST

THE FIRST CHANGE I made was not to reveal the amount of money I was earning at the nursing home. I kept some of the money, knowing it would come in useful sooner or later. However, Jean continued to collect my nursing pay. It was so embarrassing her turning up at the hospital ward in front of my colleagues. One girl even asked, "Is that your mother coming for your pay Marie?" "She's not my mother," I snapped back, totally mortified. When I got home that evening I asked Jean angrily, "Can you not wait for the money until I get home?" But of course another argument ensued and she was back up at the hospital next pay day. I just couldn't win.

In 1986 Jean did something that shocked even me. I had come on duty one evening and was working away when Sister Lynn, my ward manager, summoned me to her office. My thoughts immediately turned to Tommy, thinking perhaps he had taken a turn, or maybe a patient had made a complaint.

"Sit down Nurse Rogers," Sister Lynn ordered and on doing so, I noticed my friend Patricia sitting beside her. Patricia was a Senior Staff Nurse whom I had worked with for some time and we got very well. I looked from one to the other, wondering what was going on, until Sister Lynn asked, "Nurse Rogers; a member of the public has phoned to say that you are moonlighting and have been for some time. Is that true?" My heart started thumping. Was I about to be struck off the nursing register? After a few moments I answered nervously, "Well eh yes I am. Who phoned?" I already knew the answer, the only person who knew about my moonlighting was Jean! My thoughts were soon confirmed when Sister Lynn continued, "The matron who received the call said that it was a lady who seemed quite breathless on the phone." How could she stoop so low as to report me, when the money I earned was going into her pocket and paying her bills? It didn't make sense.

Sister Lynn finally added, "Nurse Rogers, what you do outside of this hospital is your business as long as it doesn't affect any of your nursing duties. And I have no issues with your work." Thankfully I had worked very well with Sister Lynn since completing my Orthopaedic Diploma and always worked hard. God knows what the sister was actually thinking when she was contacted by a person who had nothing else to do but get me into trouble. Fortunately for me, Jean's nasty scheme didn't work and that evening I didn't mention it and neither did she. However, she did ask me how work was that day, which was unusual considering she'd never shown any interest before. "Oh, like any other day, busy," I replied lightly and that was the end of the conversation.

A few weeks later Jean was admitted to the Belfast City Hospital with one of her asthmatic attacks. The following morning, I was called to Sister Lynn's office again. What now? I thought apprehensively as I entered the room. "You aren't allowed to receive phone calls while on duty Nurse Rogers," she said and passed the phone over to me. Puzzled, I took the phone and heard a female voice ask, "Is this Marie Rogers?" "Yes it is," I answered quietly. The voice continued, "I am Doctor Ellen, a psychiatrist in ward 7 at the City Hospital. I have been asked by the medical team to do a psychiatric assessment on Jean." Psychiatrist, I thought before answering her calmly, "Doctor Ellen, you don't need to get my permission to do an assessment on Jean, she's an adult in her own right." I was shocked when she responded with, "I am being watched by this lady as I speak to you Nurse Rogers. Are you happy for me to see her?" "Of course you can see her Doctor Ellen," I answered.

I told Sister Lynn about the call and although I really wanted to tell her my whole story, I just couldn't. Sister Lynn had always been very good to me on the ward, giving me a lot of responsibility, and she kindly offered to take me to see Jean that evening. On arriving in the ward, Jean's first comment was, "I need soap; can you go to the hospital shop and get it?" "I will bring some tomorrow," I

answered, but she interrupted, "I need the bloody soap."
I felt so embarrassed in front of my ward sister that I
went and got the soap. On returning, she remarked, "You
need to ask the doctor how I am." "I don't need to ask
the doctor; you can tell me," I answered softly, hoping
she wouldn't get nasty. Sister Lynn chatted to us for a
while, then announced she had to leave for home and we
left together. After a few days Jean returned home and
resumed her control of my life.

Since leaving the orphanage I had corresponded with
Sister Elizabeth every so often. There was method in my
madness. In each of my letters I asked various questions
about my mother and other issues that I needed answers
to. I hoped that one day she would slip up and tell me
something about my parents.

In 1987, I received a letter from Sister Elizabeth that
astonished me. She informed me that my mother was in
Letterkenny Hospital. This information came from the
very person who had said to me as a child, "Don't be silly
Marie you don't have a mother." Why did she decide to
tell me otherwise now? When her revelation finally sunk
in, it frightened the wits out of me. Imagine, after 37 years
I was going to come face to face with the person who had
brought me into this world only to leave me in the hands
of strangers. I had mixed emotions about the whole thing.

The first thing I needed to sort out was how and when
I would visit my mother. I wanted to talk it through with
a friend but knew Jean would give me no privacy if I

invited someone over. If anyone called to the house, she always sat in the parlour throughout and used various excuses to get me out of the room, such as "go and make the tea Marie" or "put the dogs out in the yard Marie". The visits were very awkward and usually I couldn't wait for my friends to leave.

I decided the best thing would be to meet a friend away from the house, so a few days later I took the dogs for their usual walk and called to the flat where Patricia lived. I asked if she wanted to go for a walk with me, she agreed and off we went. We walked for about an hour and chatted about anything and everything. I began to open up and tell her about my background but she stopped me mid-sentence, "Marie, Jean has told us all about you, I am sorry." I was shocked but not overly surprised. Patricia quickly added, "It doesn't change my view on you in any way Marie, don't worry about it."

I told her about the letter and Patricia came up with a great idea, "You could ring the hospital from the nurses's home to find out about your mother Marie," she suggested "If and when I visit Letterkenny, will you come with me?" I asked nervously. "Yes, that's no problem," she said as we arrived home. It was the longest walk the dogs had ever had!

Late one evening I plucked up the courage to ring Letterkenny Hospital. It's a phone call I'll never forget. I phoned directory enquiry, rang the hospital and eventually got through to a ward. After a few rings a voice said, "Ward C, can I help you?" I took a deep breath before answering, "Oh how is Mrs Josephine Rogers?" "Who is calling?" the nurse asked briskly. I felt sick but after another deep breath replied, "It's just a friend." I was terrified that the nurse might ask further questions but she answered right away, "Mrs Rogers is in good spirits and her health is quite good lately." "Thank you," I said quickly and put the phone down. "Wow!" I said aloud, standing alone in the hospital corridor. That was the beginning of many phone calls to the hospital over the coming months. All of them were made late in the evening after coming off duty.

At home, life was becoming unbearable with Tommy and Jean. I realised I had to tell someone that they were ruining my life, so one day I plucked up the courage to visit my GP, Dr Lewis. I hoped that if I told him what was happening at home he might understand my predicament. I was horrified to discover that Jean had been to see him the previous day and had told him I wasn't pulling my weight with them at home. During our conversation he referred me as Jean's daughter. "Dr Lewis, I am not Jean's daughter," I said. I was gobsmacked by his next comment, "My goodness, we are going to be left with the problem now."

One cold evening in late October 1987, an incident occurred that was to change everything. I had arrived home late after playing a badminton tournament to find Jean waiting at the gate as usual, arms folded across her chubby chest like a sergeant major. I was barely out of the car when she started roaring down the street, "Where the bloody hell have you been to this time? The dogs haven't been walked today."

Something inside me snapped. I walked right up to her, looked her straight in the eye and yelled, "Jean you have ruined my life for the past 20 years and I'm not prepared to take any more of it. You walk the damn dogs." I was surprised by my own outburst and was trembling all over but before she had a chance to respond, I continued, "Look Jean I think the best thing for both of us is for me to leave, because the longer I am under your spell the less chance I have of a normal life. I don't think I would be responsible for my actions if I lived with you another day." Her response startled me, "Oh yes! The best thing you can do is get the hell out of here and don't come back." Suddenly, like a Jekyll and Hyde, she changed her mind, "Look I'll give you one more chance." But this time I wasn't giving in. I turned away from her and headed straight for my bedroom.

"I told you to get out! And tell that to your nursing friends," she shouted after me. At that point, all I wanted to do was get as far away as possible from this unstable woman. I began packing the few items I had and wondered what bed I would be crying in that night when Jean came barging into the room. She started snatching things from me saying, "That isn't yours. You're not taking that." She stood right in front of me, up in my personal space, just as Sister Luke had done so often in the orphanage, "Don't forget, you came here with nothing and you can go with nothing." She kept grabbing things and after a while I just left the stuff on the bed and walked out of the room. However, there was one thing I did want and that was the little Tyrone Crystal basket I had been given as a gift on leaving the cardiac ward. As I opened the small cabinet to remove it, Jean demanded, "What the hell are you doing?" "I am taking what is mine," I replied but she grabbed it from my hand shouting, "What's in this house stays in this house!" I just looked at the pathetic woman, lifted the car keys from the hall table and walked out of the house.

She followed me out to the car and while I placed the few items I had into the boot, she ranted on, "Oh don't worry, I'm not out to wave goodbye. I'm checking you haven't stolen anything." I looked her straight in the eye and said, "The car is one thing you won't have," and with that I drove off. Glancing in the rear view mirror, I saw her standing on the pavement with her arms folded and wondered what she thought of losing both a slave and a taxi driver. While all this was taking place, Tommy stayed in the sitting room and didn't say a word, but the dogs barked like mad. God knows, maybe the poor animals sensed something was amiss.

After 21 years of hell, I was finally free and although I had absolutely nowhere to go, I didn't care. I drove around for some time wondering where on earth to go, until finally I thought of Patricia. It was well after midnight when I rang her bell several times. Mary, another nurse I knew, eventually opened the door. She and Patricia had trained together and were very close friends. "My God, Marie what has happened you?" she asked, looking worried. I guess I must have looked quite a sight, standing there with a large bin bag full of my few belongings. "Mary, would you mind if I stayed here for a few days? I know Patricia is here and there isn't enough room for somebody else, but let me stay until I get a place of my own?" Without hesitation Mary opened the door wide, "Come on in Marie, of course you can stay."

I told Patricia and Mary what had happened, and after getting me a cup of tea, they organised a sleeping area in the sitting room. I was exhausted but with so much going on in my mind, I couldn't sleep. However, for the first time in years I didn't shed a tear that night! My last thought that night was what would people think of me for leaving this elderly couple?

It was very hard to settle in Mary's house because of the closeness to Jean's home. Jean knew I was friendly with the girls and also where they lived, so I wasn't surprised when she came knocking on their door. Of course that wasn't enough for Jean, she also took to shouting through the letterbox, "I know you're in there!" I was mortified. When this didn't get a reaction, Jean started phoning Mary's house every night. It didn't matter what time it was and some nights she rang between 2.00 and 3.00 am. Her nuisance calls continued for some weeks until eventually Mary answered the phone, telling her to stop and that I wasn't living there any longer. Unfortunately, my car gave me away. Most nights I would arrive home from work and less than an hour later, Jean was shouting through the letterbox.

Determined that Jean's behaviour wouldn't get to me, I continued working and even started evening classes. The next step was to find my own accommodation, preferably as far away from Jean as possible. At the time Patricia was also attending evening classes, so we always travelled together but one evening another friend, Jenny, asked for a lift as her car had broken down. All three of us set off to our class and on the way home Patricia approached the subject of my accommodation. Jenny nursed at the same hospital and we knew each other from the badminton club. I didn't know her as well as Patricia, but when I asked if she knew of a place, she replied without hesitation, "I have a room in my house, which you can have until you find a place of your own." I was so delighted to be offered somewhere to stay well away from Jean.

The following week at the badminton club Jenny approached me, "Marie you can move into my home any time." We chatted as we waited our turn to play badminton and discovered we had more in common than we thought. "Where do you come from Marie?" Jenny asked with interest. "Oh I grew up in Belfast," I answered hoping others in the hall didn't hear me. "My sister-in-law grew up in Belfast too," she said, "maybe you know her." "What do you call her?" I asked politely, never thinking for a moment that I would actually know who she was talking about. When she told me her sister-in-law's name, you could have knocked me down with a feather. She was one of the girls from the orphanage and one I knew very well. She had left the orphanage some years before me, so we had lost touch but I remembered her fondly.

Jenny was as excited as I was to learn that we had something in common. From then on a great friendship was formed between us and a few days later I moved what little stuff I had in my black bin liner into Jenny's house.

I shall never forget that first night in Jenny's house. Everything was so strange simply because I wasn't used to being showered with such kindness. We sat chatting for a few hours, until Jenny eventually said, "Marie, do you want to go to bed? I will show you your room." "Are you sure?" I asked, so used to being the last to bed after living with Tommy and Jean. I found it difficult to make my own decisions after so many years of being told what to do but Jenny seemed to understand, knowing the kind of life her sister-in-law endured. She was a really good friend to me.

Despite Jenny's kindness I felt a little deflated and lonely that night. I took some time to gather my thoughts but I tried to keep positive and focus on the future. The following morning I woke to the smell of a fry cooking and, amazingly, I had slept like a baby. I was still getting used to not being called during the night to Jean's commands. While having our breakfast, I turned to Jenny and said, "My bed was very warm thank you, what was that thing you put in the bed that was hot?" She looked at me in amazement, "It was a hot water bottle; did you not know that?" I was embarrassed, "I'm not used to having my bed warmed, breakfast ready, and offering to do my washing. Thank you so much." "It's about time somebody pampered you," she replied. "Do you want me to clean the house?" I asked but was interrupted, "Don't even think of it. You are not here to clean. Just focus on getting yourself sorted out and that is what matters to me."

There were days I didn't know what to do with myself after getting home from work. I was so used to cleaning, walking the dogs and caring for Tommy and Jean. Now I could come home from work, read the paper, and even be happy with my own company. Previously, I would have been reminded by Jean that there was no time to read the paper. Most importantly, I didn't have to say what I was doing or where I was going. After a while, I even stopped expecting Jean to be waiting for me down the street. What I was now experiencing was absolute bliss!

It was difficult understanding Jenny's generosity and kindness but thankfully over the weeks I learnt to accept it. I began to enjoy her big-heartedness and the freedom I was experiencing for the very first time in 37 years.

At night Jenny would be in her bedroom and I in mine and we would talk into each other's room for hours.

"How would you like to hear another story?" I'd ask, rambling on. It felt like there was something building up inside me and it was escaping in small bubbles. I opened up to this kind woman, wanting to share my terrible experiences and revealed a lot of stuff from my past about the orphanage, the lodgings and the individuals who had ruined my life to date. I soon realised that there were people in the world who cared about other people and I found it so reassuring.

One evening, Jenny and I were chatting over dinner when she commented, "Marie, why don't you write a book about your experiences? I think it would help even for therapeutic and emotional reasons." "You must be joking Jenny," I answered laughing, "How on earth could I write a book with my lack of education?" "Nothing is impossible," she replied.

I understood what she was saying but I also knew it would be a huge challenge for me and reliving the past 37 years could be very traumatic. I would have to think long and hard about revealing my background to the public. Would people think less of me for exposing what I, along with my friends, had to endure in the orphanage and beyond?

I continued to enjoy the complete freedom and support my friends were giving me and hoped it would last forever. However, after many months with Jenny I began to feel uneasy, not because I didn't enjoy the comforts of a good home but because I was afraid that Jean would find out where Jenny lived and would do the same as she did with Mary. I just didn't want that to happen.

While nursing at the private nursing home I found out that there was a small, empty bed-sit and asked if I could rent it. The bed-sit was like an outbuilding at the end of the nursing home. What appealed to me was that it was in Carryduff and that was certainly out of Jean's reach. Thankfully, after a long chat, Jenny accepted my decision and had no objection to me moving on. My nursing friends all rallied round and helped me move. This was the first time I had lived by myself and the bed-sit proved quite a lonely place. It was quite basic, consisting of one large room, with a bed in the corner and a shower room attached. It definitely hadn't the same comforts of Jenny's home.

One day at work I mentioned to Sister Lynn about the bed-sit I was living in and she suggested I contact the Housing Executive. I had never heard of them so she rang on my behalf to see if I could get accommodation with them. "Why don't you ring your GP to see if he would write to the Housing Executive to support you?"she said. I explained my GP's response when I said I was leaving Tommy and Jean, so Sister Lynn again offered to ring for me but received no help from the GP. I waited a few months before contacting the Housing Executive and was eventually offered accommodation in Finaghy.

I fell in love with the little flat at once. At 38 years of age I was going to have a place that I could call home for the first time and I was ecstatic. I was so looking forward to living on my own, in my own flat, where I could do anything I wanted without being told, "Don't do this and don't do that!" I was going to be my own boss! When I moved into the little flat, I decorated it to suit me and it really felt like home. Everything was going well and I was so happy with life but it wasn't to last.

One night after 11.00 pm the telephone rang. "Hello," I answered it with a sleepy voice. No reply. "Hello! Who's this?" I asked again. No response. I held the receiver for a few seconds, when suddenly, I realised to my horror who it was. I threw the phone down on the chair, frozen on the spot. The person at the other end of the phone didn't have to speak; it was the breathlessness that gave her away. Jean had my number and I was terrified. "How the heck did she know my number?" I asked myself, starting to shake.

I tried not to let Jean worry me but after the second and third call she started to get to me. The calls were eerie; she never spoke but her breathing said it all. If she knew my phone number there was also a chance that she knew my address and that frightened me the most. At least on the phone I had her at arm's length but to come face to face with her again would be a different matter.

During one of her voiceless calls I screamed down the phone, "I know it's you Jean, get out of my life and leave me alone for good!" Like the previous calls she would slam the phone down and the following day I had my number changed. Unfortunately that didn't deter her and weeks later the phone rang about 3.00 am. Startled from my sleep I jumped and lifted the phone without thought and again there was silence. Jean again! When was I going to see the end of this woman who was determined to annoy me in every way possible?

The following night brought the same, but I refused to answer. I stood looking at the phone, listening to it ring until eventually I could stand it no longer. I lifted the receiver with every intention of screaming down the line, only to hear Patricia's voice. What a relief I thought.

"Marie, I am sorry for contacting you at this time of the night. I think you should know that Tommy is very ill in the City Hospital." "How did you hear Patricia?" I asked shocked. "Joan is nursing him and it was Tommy's brother-in-law Brian who asked that you be informed." Joan was another of my nursing friends who was working at the City Hospital. "Patricia, there's no way I am going down there to face that woman. She has been phoning for a while and not saying a word, but I know it's her," I replied. "Marie, Brian said Tommy won't make it through the night and he will get Jean home, so you won't meet her at the hospital." There was a pause before Patricia continued, "Marie I will go to the hospital with you." I gave in, "Well, OK I will meet you at the hospital entrance shortly."

After getting to the ward, Joan lead us to Tommy's bed but I found myself looking down at a skeleton. The change in this man after a period of just six months was alarming. He was unrecognisable and literally dying in front of my eyes. I was petrified. How the heck did he get to this stage? Was I responsible? "That's not the Tommy I knew," I whispered to Patricia. His brother-in-law came into the ward with his wife and stood at the other side of the bed. They didn't speak and the silence was deafening. You could cut the atmosphere with a knife until, after a few minutes, Patricia spoke, "I think we should let Marie have time with Tommy, don't you?" I glanced at her and watched as they all left the room.

I sat in shock for a few minutes, staring at this dying man and saying to myself, if only things were different. After a few seconds I moved closer to Tommy and whispered into his ear, "You can go to sleep now its Marie here. I am doing fine." I sat back in the chair and suddenly he took one long, last breath and that was it. "Oh God He's dead!" I shouted, with tears streaming down my face. The nurse came rushing in with Tommy's brother-in-law, his wife and Patricia in tow. I was lead out of the ward shaking and crying. I should have been relieved for Tommy, who was now out of his misery but it was the dreadful state that Tommy was in that shook me to the core. He was so emaciated.

Patricia took me into the office where Joan asked us to wait for the doctor. A short time later the door opened and a tall lady wearing a white doctor's coat entered the room. On looking up at her I realised I knew her. I had worked with her at Musgrave Park Hospital and was embarrassed that she had seen the state of Tommy. I hope she doesn't think I had something to do with his illness, I thought, as she told us about Tommy's condition.

"How on God's earth did he get into such a state?" I asked quietly. The doctor explained that Tommy had been transferred from Windsor House Psychiatric Unit that morning, where he had been admitted a week earlier for attempting to kill his wife. Everything went into slow motion and I felt faint. Sliding lower into the seat I was shocked to hear that Tommy was in the very unit where I had spent some months in 1968/9.

"Are you alright Marie?" Patricia asked. I just nodded my head and the doctor continued, "Apparently, it was because of you that he lashed out at his wife." "No way would he do that!" I cried at her, "Who told you he tried to kill his wife?" To which she replied as kindly as she could, "The psychiatrist stated that on Tommy's admission his wife told the staff that Tommy tried to kill her with the kitchen knife." I was knocked for six hearing this and could only say, "This just isn't true."

There was nothing more I could say or do now to change what had happened, so Patricia and I began to head home. On the way out of the hospital we met Tommy's brother-in-law again. He spoke briefly to me, saying that they knew I had moved on and had my own life. They tried to contact me about Tommy's illness but didn't know where to find me.

Tommy was buried a few days later and I had to complete my final duty by attending, along with a few of my nursing friends. This was done in the peace of the church, long before Jean or any of his family arrived.

A few weeks later I had an urge to visit Tommy's grave as a final mark of respect. I rang his brother-in-law to find out where the grave was but when my friend and I arrived at the graveyard, we couldn't find it. We asked the graveyard staff for help but believe it or not they couldn't find it either. It was a weird experience to say the least and I never returned.

One day I bumped into an old neighbour who lived near Jean on the Lisburn Road. She shot over to me, asking how I was and where I was living. I kept our conversation very brief, conscious not to reveal where I was living and as I moved away from her she shouted after me, "You shouldn't have left Tommy and Jean. Those people took you in from the orphanage." My heart sank hearing her mention the orphanage but I wasn't overly surprised by her reaction.

On the same day I met another lady, called Sadie, who lived just three doors from Jean. I saw her from a distance and immediately thought, oh God not another sermon. But I needn't have worried. Sadie's reaction was very different. She came running over to me and genuinely seemed delighted to see me. She told me with sincerity, "Marie if only I had known you came from an orphanage and the way Jean treated you, I would have adopted you years ago." My goodness, that woman must have told all the neighbours about me. Anyway, we chatted for some time and exchanged telephone numbers. Sadie was a lovely, friendly woman but very private, with only her two sons on her mind. One son later moved to England but the other remained in Belfast and worked as a hairdresser. I promised to keep in touch with her and did until she sadly died.

Months later I met yet another neighbour from the Lisburn Road. Like Sadie, Bridie was delighted to see me. She lived at the end of the street and had often said hello as I passed with the dogs and when I was out painting the railings around the garden. She lived alone and worked as a Care Assistant in the hospital I worked in. "Have you seen your mother since she visited you Marie?" she asked politely. "How did you know my mother visited me Bridie?" I asked, knowing of course that I had never met my mother. "Jean said your mother came to see you and that she was very glamorous and wealthy," she answered. "I never saw my mother Bridie," I finished.

As we parted company I thought back to the night I left Jean's home and how she prevented me from taking a lot of my personal belongings, including the few letters I had received from the solicitor. On leaving that night I actually couldn't find any of the letters. I quizzed Jean many times about things going missing but never seemed to get anywhere with her.

Chapter Eight

THE MEETING

IN 1988 THE TIME seemed right to visit my mother in Letterkenny Hospital. I arranged to meet up with a friend called Margaret who came from Rathlin Island, which is near Ballycastle. We both nursed at Musgrave Park Hospital and socialised together. While having coffee I told Margaret what my plan was and asked if she would travel to the hospital with Patricia and I, to which she agreed, "Give me plenty of notice so that I can get the day off."

As I waited for the two girls to get back to me with a day that suited them both, I began to mentally prepare for the meeting. It was an emotional time and I often wondered if all this stress would be worth it. But although the word 'rejection' regularly entered my thoughts, I was fiercely driven by the need to know who I really was.

On a cold, brisk afternoon in early March, the three of us set off to Letterkenny Hospital and the most important visit of my life. I hadn't slept well the night before, with so many questions running through my mind. I had tried writing them down but they didn't seem to make sense in black and white, so I ripped up the page before falling asleep.

As I drove from one town to another, my friends did their best to keep the conversation going. I was so engrossed in my own thoughts that I heard very little and certainly didn't appreciate the scenic views. As we neared Donegal, my heart began to beat faster and faster until Margaret interrupted my thoughts, "We're here folks. There's the sign for the Hospital." "My God, it's 4.00 pm. Will they let us in?" I asked nervously. "Don't worry Marie. We'll get in one way or the other," Patricia reassured me, as I parked in the huge car park.

"Oh my God I'm dreading this. Do you think she'll recognise me? What'll I do if she doesn't want to see me?" I spluttered as I entered the hospital. "Marie you can only hope for the best, things will be fine," Margaret answered confidently. "Let's go and find the ward before it gets any later," said Patricia, setting off down a seemingly endless corridor. I followed uneasily.

A voice asked from a distance, "Can I help you please?" Margaret nudged me to respond to the question. I coughed to clear my throat, "We'd like to see Mrs Rogers please." But before the lady had time to reply I added, "We've travelled all the way from Belfast and we're not sure of your visiting times." "That's no problem," the receptionist answered pleasantly, "I'll have to inform the ward that you are here, have a seat please."

As we sat down I took in my surroundings. The hospital looked Victorian and was in need of a lick of paint. It reminded me of the orphanage and I had a flashback of scrubbing a stone floor similar to the one beneath my feet. I must have looked worried because Margaret asked me, "Are you alright Marie?" "I wonder who scrubs these floors," I whispered back. We waited so long that I became quite fidgety. "What's keeping them?" I mumbled, "Surely it couldn't take all this time to contact a ward." A few minutes later the receptionist walked over and apologised for the delay.

She directed us to the ward and the sign above the door stopped me dead in my tracks. In large print the sign read 'Psycho-Geriatric Unit'. My voice quivered, "Look Patricia, see that sign?" I gripped her arm tightly, "For God's sake, we're in the wrong place. Let's get out of here!" But I was interrupted by a jolly voice, "Can I help you?" The three of us turned to see a tall, rosy-cheeked nurse approaching. "Oh hello, we are here to see Mrs Rogers please," Margaret said politely. "Of course you can see her," the nurse replied brightly and escorted us half way up the ward. She stopped beside a very old, frail lady, sitting in an armchair.

As I looked around, I noticed that even the ward looked Victorian. There were about 20 beds on either side, some occupied and some empty. "I think we're in the wrong place," I said to nobody in particular. I was feeling nauseous and had an overwhelming urge to run.

Patricia sensed my fear and said convincingly, "Maybe the ordinary ward was busy Marie, so your mother had to come into this one."

The nurse left us and I murmured, "Which one is she?" "There Marie, that's your mother. You have her features," Margaret replied gently. I stared down at the woman who had brought me into this unforgiving world. She was very old and frail, with aged skin. She didn't seem to know we were there and stared into space. I felt incredibly uncomfortable and didn't want to believe that this woman in the psycho-geriatric ward was my mother.

Margaret touched my arm gently, "Here Marie, sit beside your mother." I looked at her in amazement; sitting beside this woman was the last thing I wanted to do. Reluctantly I moved closer and we all sat down, Margaret and Patricia on one side of the armchair and I on the other. Suddenly, a voice began shouting from the other end of the ward, "Eileen, Eileen, is that you?" We looked at each other. "Eileen, is that you?" the voice said again, drawing nearer. It was coming from a confused looking lady who was walking up the ward. "Who's she talking to?" I asked the girls, who looked at each other before Margaret called back, "I think you have the wrong person." But the lady continued to walk towards us.

My heart was beating so fast that I thought I was going to collapse. "Marie, look at the woman," Patricia said quietly but it was only when the lady came to the side of my chair that I glanced up and realised how confused she looked. "Oh my goodness, I am sorry, but I thought you were someone I know," she mumbled hesitantly. I said nothing.

The lady remained standing beside us, so Margaret asked her, "We knew this woman many years ago. Did you know her well?" Please God let her go away, I thought but to my astonishment the woman replied, "Och sure didn't I work for her for many years. Many cups of soup she gave me during the cold winter days. She was a fine looking woman and liked by the whole community." As the lady spoke she stared at me, as though speaking to me directly. I couldn't believe what this woman was revealing.

"You know she had the three children don't you?" she continued. "Oh yes that's right," answered Margaret quickly. "Does her family still visit?" Patricia asked. "Oh Goodness me, of course they do," the woman rambled on, "Sure her daughters and nieces come often to see her. And her niece cuts her hair from time to time." I must have half-sisters, I thought excitedly.

I let Margaret and Patricia do all the talking, while I listened intently. Although still very anxious I was delighted with all this new information. After some time a nurse shouted from outside the office, "Mrs Hogan, will you please come for your tablets?" When I realised the nurse was calling the lady beside us, I whispered to my friends, "Damn it she's a patient!" "Maybe it's as well Marie," Margaret answered. "Do you think she really knew my mother?" I asked uncertainly. "I would think so Marie. She knew too much about your mother's business," Margaret assured me. I wondered what Mrs Hogan's reaction would have been if I had told her I was Mrs Rogers's daughter.

Once Mrs Hogan was out of sight, I turned my attention back to the person in the armchair. She was extremely thin and as I crept closer, she didn't acknowledge my presence or even blink an eyelid. I felt cold all over and gripped Patricia's arm. "Jesus Christ! She's not my mother, we have the wrong person!" I hissed, my voice rising. Patricia replied gently, "Come on Marie, it is her." I rummaged in my handbag and pulled out the photograph the solicitor had given me. Pointing at it, I insisted, "Look Patricia, that's my mother, this is the person I want to see, not her." "You must understand that your mother has aged since that photo was taken. She was a young woman then Marie," Patricia said compassionately.

I looked at the ghostly figure propped up in the chair beside us and realised she would never be able to answer my questions. She was obviously suffering from Alzheimer's disease and I was really looking at a stranger, not a mother.

My friends decided to leave me alone with her. "My God, don't you go far away," I called after them. I looked back to the woman in the chair with mixed emotions. I wanted to shake her and yell, "Why did you do this to me?" But I wanted to hug her too. I felt completely overwhelmed.

I didn't know what to do with myself. How does a child get close to her mother after 38 years? I drew closer, touched her gently on the shoulder, then pulled my hand away. Oh my God this is terrible, I thought, moving back. When she didn't respond I gently touched her again but this time I also whispered in her ear, "It's me Marie Therese, your daughter." I looked around the ward hoping nobody heard me. After a few seconds she turned her head towards me. To my surprise she looked straight at me and muttered, "Jesus, Mary and Joseph!" before turning her head upwards. I almost fell off the seat. Sadly, these were the first and only words my mother spoke to me.

I beckoned my two friends over. "I can't take anymore of this, let's get out of this place," I blurted out. "Are you alright Marie?" Margaret asked. My reply was barely audible, "Jesus! She just spoke to me." My friends looked at each other. "You must have triggered something in the recesses of her mind," Patricia explained. "Why didn't she say more to me?" I mumbled in a state of shock, crying at the same time.

Eventually my friends guided me out of the ward. At the door, I looked over my shoulder towards the figure sitting in the armchair and nodded my head in despair. I also glanced over at Mrs Hogan who had told us so much. Her eyes followed us until we were out of sight.

I was emotionally shattered by the visit. Walking towards the car, Margaret gently took the car keys from me, "I will drive home Marie. You're in no fit state to drive." I didn't object. I couldn't even hold the car keys properly.

The journey home was a complete haze. At one point I realised I was still holding the photograph of my mother, which was wet with my tears. I recalled the first time tears had fallen on the picture, in the factory all those years ago. I was suddenly furious that Sister Elizabeth hadn't told me about my mother sooner. Who told her about my mother? How long had she known about her illness? I asked myself these questions over and over again but I was 60 years old before I got some answers.

I continued ringing Letterkenny Hospital at every opportunity. One evening while making enquiries I asked the nurse, "Has anybody come to visit her lately?" To which she replied breezily, "Sure, her brother was here just today from Donegal." After replacing the receiver I shouted with excitement, "Oh my God, I have an uncle!" As my voice reverberated around my tiny flat, I had to steady myself. The lady in the flat below would think I had gone completely mad! It was beyond belief that the nurse had inadvertently provided my uncle's name and the area he lived in.

My search was far from over but I was determined to continue. A few days later I put pen to paper and wrote to my uncle in Donegal. I didn't know what to say or how to say it. I didn't even know his exact address but I took a chance and posted the letter to the address I heard the nurse mention. Even though there was no house number, I was prepared to take that chance. The following is what I remember writing:

"Dear Sir

I hope you don't mind me writing to you. My name is Marie Therese Rogers and I think I am your sister's daughter. I have been secretly visiting her in the Letterkenny Hospital for some time. I grew up in Nazareth House Orphanage in Belfast. A nun informed me some months ago that my mother was in hospital. I would appreciate if you could let me know if you are related to Mrs Josephine Rogers and if so would love to make contact with you. Forgive me for imposing upon you but I am very keen to discover who I am and my identity.

Yours faithfully"

I sat looking over the letter for some time, thinking how do I sign it? I wanted to sign it "your niece", but I couldn't. The walk to the post box seemed lengthy and on reaching it I hesitated before actually placing the letter in the red box. As I did so, I said aloud, "Please God, let it be the right person." Isn't it strange how people turn to God for spiritual guidance when they want something special to happen in their lives?

To my delight, I received a reply three days later. As I lifted the letter from the letterbox, I knew it was from my uncle by the South of Ireland postmark. My hands were shaking so much that I could barely hold the envelope but I needn't have worried, the letter contained only words that I wanted to hear.

He explained who he was and that his sister was indeed in Letterkenny Hospital, and had been there for many years. He expressed his shock on hearing she had a daughter he knew nothing about but at the time of my birth he was a doctor in England. He went on to say how he had contacted the orphanage to find out if I had actually been there. Initially I was annoyed and wondered if he didn't believe me but he went on to say that we could meet. I was ecstatic.

He suggested we meet between Derry and Belfast and asked me to bring any documents I had as proof of who I was. A date, venue and time were given, which could be changed if unsuitable. To my surprise he ended the letter "Your Aunt and Uncle."

I sat holding the letter, now wet from tears and began to read it over and over again. As the realisation of finally making contact with a member of my own family was beginning to sink in, I jumped up, throwing the letter in the air and shouting, "Yippee! At last I have found my family."

This was the break I had waited for and I only wished my orphan friends could be with me to experience my excitement. The horrible word 'rejection' was suddenly replaced with words like 'belonging' and 'achievement'.

The jigsaw was finally fitting into place.

I was of course quite nervous about meeting these strangers. I spent several sleepless nights, my mind racing and full of questions: Will I meet their expectations? Will they react in the same way that my mother did? Had I caused a family feud by revealing myself? How will they react when they discover I'm not properly educated? What will they think when they find out I've had a breakdown?

To distract myself, I focused on what I would wear for the meeting because as the old saying goes, first impressions always stick. I bought a beautiful navy suit with a white blouse. Arrangements were made for us to meet at the Everglades Hotel on the Derry/Belfast road. I was excited but didn't want to go on my own, so again I turned to my friend Margaret for support. She agreed and said she wanted to do some shopping in Derry anyway, so would leave us to it.

The day finally arrived on a fresh September morning in 1988. Margaret drove and we set off early, after I checked I had all the necessary documents one last time. "What if they don't turn up Margaret?" I asked, my palms sweating. "Marie, don't even think of that. Of course they'll turn up. Remember they'll be as anxious and apprehensive as you are," she replied. I relaxed a little after that and we chatted the whole way. Before I knew it, we were driving into the hotel car park. "Do I look respectable enough?" I asked, starting to panic. "You look really well," Margaret reassured me.

There wasn't a soul about as we made our way to the hotel reception and of course I immediately thought they weren't coming, "Oh God there's nobody here." "Marie it's too early," Margaret said soothingly. I was becoming flustered, "Let's go to the ladies quickly. I want to make sure I am presentable before they arrive." I straightened myself out quickly and in my hurry ripped my tights! "Now what am I going to do?" I squeaked, but when I looked at Margaret I burst out laughing. There was nothing for it but to try and hide the hole with my handbag. We went back to the foyer and sat watching people come and go, my nerves increasing with every second.

At 3.00 pm, an anxious-looking couple arrived and Margaret nudged me, "I think that's them Marie!" I froze, feeling sick with fear. As they approached, I took in every detail. The man was quite tall, with receding hair and wore a smart suit and overcoat. He had some of my mother's features, including her high cheekbones and I instinctively knew we must be related. His wife was smaller, with neatly-styled grey hair and wore an Irish tweed suit.

I'm looking at a blood relation, I thought, almost bursting with joy. "Are you Marie Therese?" the man asked softly. I was so overcome that I couldn't even answer him. Margaret spoke for me, "Yes, this is Marie Therese and I am Margaret, her friend." We stood up and exchanged greetings, and I noticed my uncle's handshake was warm, just like his manner.

My uncle motioned for us to sit down and Margaret explained that she was leaving us to do some shopping. My uncle spoke to the receptionist and shortly afterwards tea and biscuits arrived. His wife poured the tea and we started chatting. I was quite relieved that we were the only people in the foyer at that moment because I didn't want strangers hearing our conversation.

I produced the documents for my uncle to read, after which he looked at me and said, "You certainly resemble your mother. Looking at you, I can see my sister in her younger days." My mouth was dry but I managed to smile and said, "Do you think so?" My hands were sweating again and the teacup shook as I held it. My uncle told me several times that I had no need to be so nervous.

My uncle did most of the talking to begin with but I noticed his wife had an English accent. He asked about me and what life was like in the orphanage and after that. As I told him my story, I felt tears trickle down my face. I glanced up at his wife and she too was dabbing her eyes with a tissue. Even my uncle's eyes were glazed with unshed tears by the time I had finished. It was a very emotional meeting for us all.

As the hours passed, I learned that I had two half-sisters and a half-brother. I remembered the lady in the hospital who thought I was someone she knew and I realised I must resemble one of the half-sisters. My uncle told me quite a bit about my mother and the hotel she ran for years following the death of her husband. I recalled that the solicitor told me my mother had a business.

My head was buzzing with all this information, yet the more I heard the more I wanted to know. I didn't ask too many questions because I was happy simply listening to what my uncle had to say but I felt quite at ease with this couple, my long lost family.

I eventually told them about my phone calls and secret visits to the hospital. I also explained how the solicitor visited the factory in 1968 and produced the small photograph of my mother. My uncle appeared quite shocked by this. He and his wife looked at the photograph, then at each other before returning it to me. "Hopefully you will have more photographs of your mother and the family," my uncle said earnestly, his wife nodding in agreement.

I didn't want them to leave but like all good things, the meeting had to come to an end. Margaret returned after a few hours and my uncle said that he and his wife must start their journey home. As he put his coat on he said, "Marie Therese, we will be in touch with you soon. We want to inform our family of the meeting first."

I was left wondering if they would organise another meeting and on the way to the car park asked Margaret, "Do you think they'll want to meet me again?" "We can only wait and hope Marie," she replied. I really hope so, I thought on the way home but if not, it was a meeting I would certainly never forget.

Weeks later I received a letter inviting me to my uncle's home for a weekend. I had come this far, so I accepted his invite. The closer I got to the visit the more excited I became. I wanted the whole world to know that I was no longer an orphan and contacted as many of the Nazareth girls as I could to tell them my good news.

One October morning I set off on my visit alone. As the early sun glinted through the cold October clouds I felt myself brimming over with excitement. The day felt full of possibilities and the scenery seemed to reflect this optimism. The trees were displaying their autumn colours in all their splendour, and as I drove along, I wondered if my meeting would be as colourful.

I had no difficulty following my uncle's instructions and although I had to stop a few times to ease the back pain I had been experiencing since 1982, I arrived at my destination within an hour and a half. My uncle's house was large and stood on its own over-looking a golf course. I sat outside its gates for a few minutes to compose my thoughts and was relieved to see my uncle's name on the wall in front of the house. I was definitely at the right place.

As I walked up the path towards the door, I saw my aunt standing on the porch to greet me. My heart was thumping and my hands were sweating again. She welcomed me to their home and showed me into their sitting room, which was full of beautiful pictures. "Perhaps you would like to unpack Marie Therese," my uncle spoke as he entered the room. I agreed and my aunt showed me to the bedroom, where she left me to unpack my few items, "Come back to the sitting room when you're ready Marie Therese." I stretched my back to ease the pain and stood thinking, what have I let myself in for?

On returning to the sitting room I could smell freshly baked scones and I was ready for them. While politely sipping tea I listened to my uncle talk about his children, how well they had all done and what they were doing now. I have nieces and nephews, I thought, as I listened intently, not wanting to miss a thing. I felt much more relaxed this time. I told them more about the orphanage and my life since leaving it but tried to steer the conversation towards my nursing. I was uncomfortable discussing my education in case they thought less of me.

After dinner we talked some more and I was surprised by their interest in my time lodging with Tommy and Jean. As I told them about my unhappy existence after the orphanage, the tears began to flow. I kept talking, wanting to get it all out of my system. When I finally finished, I couldn't remember all that was said but I felt more at peace. My uncle looked at me compassionately, "Marie Therese, you resemble your mother. And you seem to have the same strength and determination to succeed in life, which thankfully you did."

He asked if I had any questions, so I asked if the whole family knew about me. His response was a little strange, "Well we thought it best not to tell your brother; he has a serous drink problem so hearing about you could add to his sad problem." I had a sudden flash back to my childhood when I wrote the essay about the family and the big brother I would dearly love. Going by what I had just heard there was little chance of that ever happening.

The following morning my uncle announced, "Let's go for a nice drive Marie Therese. I will show you the parts of Donegal where your roots began." During the drive he told me some bits and pieces about my mother's upbringing. I was fascinated listening to him; he had such a lovely way of explaining things. At times I closed my eyes and imagined myself growing up in a normal family environment.

During my visit I met a lady who came into my uncle's home to cook and clean. After dinner I went to help her wash the dishes. I had only left the room for a short time when my aunt called after me, "Marie Therese, you don't need to help with the dishes, Mrs Brown will do them." "Oh I don't mind helping," I replied but she insisted, "Come on don't worry Mrs Brown is used to cleaning away." I returned to the sitting room and after a few minutes she asked, "Did Mrs Brown ask who you were?" "No she didn't," I replied and she continued, "Did you tell her anything?" "No" I said, feeling a little uncomfortable. "Marie Therese, we are going out but should anybody ring and ask who you are, just say you are a friend or a cousin," she finished. I now felt rather awkward and luckily nobody did ring.

Before heading back to Belfast that Sunday evening, arrangements were made for another visit and this time I would meet my two half-sisters. This excited me greatly. Would they like me or maybe even look like me? I wondered on the way home. I had heard so much over the last few days that it was hard to remember every detail but I couldn't wait to hear more.

A few months later, I was on my way back to Donegal as promised. Although I was quite comfortable with my newfound relatives, I was daunted by the prospect of meeting my half-sisters. I arrived early on a fresh afternoon and was met by my aunt who escorted me into the now familiar sitting room. We had tea and chatted before dinner. "Marie Therese your sisters should be here in time for dinner", she announced afterwards. God, I hope they're alright, I thought. As if reading my mind, my uncle said softly, "Don't worry Marie Therese you will be just fine."

We moved to the dinning room and a few minutes later, the doorbell sounded. I began to feel unsettled. "That will be your sisters," my uncle said, as my aunt and two other women entered the room. I felt quite insignificant as the three women stood over me. When I looked up, one cried out, "I don't believe it, she is so like Mark's daughter!" I was then introduced to Donna and Nancy, my half-sisters.

"Right, now, dinner is ready," my aunt called from an adjoining room. "I will give you a hand," Donna said, heading off towards the kitchen. My uncle showed us all where to sit, around a large circular table, set with a beautiful linen tablecloth and matching crockery fit for a queen. I was placed opposite my half-sisters, which gave me the opportunity to study their body language. It wasn't long before I realised they had very different personalities.

Nancy appeared much more at ease than Donna, who actually made me a little uncomfortable. I think it was because she reminded me a little of the solicitor who had visited the factory. She was tall and well dressed, with dark hair and blue eyes, and she oozed confidence. Nancy on the other hand was more like me, smaller and with dark eyes. She had our mother's features and came across as very friendly.

I didn't really enjoy the meal with so many strangers looking at me. It didn't help that every time I attempted to lift peas from the plate, the damn things ended up on the floor. After dinner we headed for the sitting room again. Questions came at me from all angles and I thought it was never going to end. I was too nervous to ask any questions of my own and instead the four of them began questioning each other. It was quite uncomfortable and I felt like I was intruding looking from one to the other. "Didn't you know that mammy was pregnant at the time?" Donna asked my uncle. "Sure how would I have known when I was away studying medicine in England at that time," he replied.

All I wanted was answers, but it didn't look like I was going to get them. I continued listening as they discussed my mother's whereabouts in the late 40s. "How on earth did mammy get to Belfast without anybody missing her?"

my aunt asked, not looking at anybody in particular. "God almighty, she must have known somebody and anyway I was away at boarding school, so I don't know the answer to that," Nancy replied.

As the evening wore on, the questions continued. I managed to ask a few simple ones of my own but didn't get any satisfying answers. My uncle turned to me at one point and asked, "Marie Therese do you know who your father is?" "I just know that his name is Denis Moloney," I answered quietly. I explained what I knew about my father and noticed my uncle looking at Donna, as though waiting for something. "Sure that would be Dinnie! Och, I'll tell you later," she whispered loudly. Now all eyes were on her. She knows more than she is letting on, I thought angrily.

"How did you find us?" she suddenly changed the topic. I told them about the visit from the solicitor, the contact I had with the nun from the orphanage and her letter telling me about my mother being in Letterkenny Hospital. "What was the solicitor's name?" my uncle asked. When I replied, I noticed Donna's expression change, "Oh wouldn't you know she would be at something." Again I sensed that Donna and Mrs White knew each other quite well.

My half-sisters asked me about the orphanage and I found it rather difficult to relive events to such a large group of people. As I told them about being sent away to school for the educationally subnormal, I noticed Nancy was crying. "Oh stop that whining," Donna snapped from the corner of the room, "It's well and fine you talking, you didn't have to endure the life Marie Therese had to." Nancy responded quite angrily and my uncle interrupted, "Now let's not get upset here, it is traumatic enough for Marie Therese."

The hours passed and dusk began to fall. The questioning slowed without me getting to the bottom of how and when my mother got to Belfast. The sisters announced they had a long journey ahead and should make tracks. My aunt saw them to the door but on the way Nancy turned to me and said, "Marie Therese you will have to come to my place for a break. I will be in touch soon." After they left, my uncle told me more about the two women and their families. My mother wasn't mentioned again.

My head was buzzing when I went to bed that night and I didn't sleep for hours. I realised I was also relieved that Donna and Nancy hadn't hugged me.

Months later, Nancy invited me to stay with her for a weekend. By this stage I was getting quite used to travelling to Donegal. Maybe I will learn more about my mother from Nancy I thought on the way. However, something happened while staying with Nancy. Very late on the second night, after we had gone to bed, I heard the phone ring several times. Nancy spoke to somebody then came into the room I was sharing with her young daughter, Norma. She whispered, "Norma the nurse has just phoned to say mammy isn't too well. I am going to the hospital, I'll be back soon." I didn't want her to know I could hear her so I lay perfectly still until she left. Why didn't she waken me? I thought.

The following morning I hoped to find out more but heard nothing until that evening. Nancy announced she and Norma were going to visit her mother in hospital. I wasn't asked to join them and the phone call during the night wasn't mentioned. I felt hurt and excluded. While they were away I wandered about the house and found it unusual that there was no evidence that my mother had ever been there. There wasn't even a photograph of her.

That wasn't the only strange thing to happen that weekend. The annual local fair was on and Nancy suggested we go. She was going to see her older daughter and was keen for me to meet her. It was a lovely bright summer's day and as I hadn't been to a fair before, I was certainly looking forward to it.

When we arrived we looked around the many stalls and chatted to Nancy's daughter. As we talked, two elderly women passed us and one turned to the other, spluttering, "My God Did you see that woman there? She's the spitting image of Josie Rogers!" The other woman looked over her shoulder at me and replied, "Merciful God, she certainly is. Who's she?" I heard the women clearly, as did Nancy, who looked back but didn't say anything. The two women walked on at a much slower pace, as though waiting to see where I was going. It ruined the day in a way, as I spent the rest of our time at the fair walking with my head down in case someone else stared at me.

As we made our way back to the car, Nancy walked on ahead, leaving her daughter and I to chat. Her daughter handed me a ring and said, "Marie Therese, see if this fits you." The ring slid onto my little finger as if made for it. "That was your mother's eternity ring," she explained, "I'd like you to have it." I was delighted and looking down at the ring, I imagined my mother wearing it as a young woman and walking along the same little Donegal village.

While having our tea that evening, Nancy told her husband about the incident at the fair, "Guess what happened today? The two Hamilton sisters that live up the road thought Marie Therese looked like Mammy." She seemed annoyed and I felt embarrassed. It reminded me of when my aunt told me to say I was a cousin when staying with them. Was I such a shame to them? I wondered while Nancy chattered on.

I got on quite well with Nancy and visited her quite a few times. She was kind to me but never mentioned the family. She did however, give me a little Hummel figurine that she said was my mother's and was given to her by my grandmother.

In 1989 I visited my aunt and uncle for what was to be the last time, although I didn't know it at the time. We had just finished dinner and were sitting listening to classical music when my uncle glanced over at his wife. He looked at me and said quietly, "Marie Therese there is something else we feel you should know about your mother." A few years before I received your letter, your Aunt Annie died. While clearing out her bungalow I found a letter from a person we didn't know who she had been communicating with. I contacted the person in the letter and a few days later received a reply. Your mother had a little girl before you were born; your sister." I froze, completely bewildered by what he had just said, and simply stared at him. I felt the colour drain from my face as I asked apprehensively. "Oh my God, what orphanage was she in?" He continued, "Fortunately, your sister wasn't in an orphanage. When your sister was born; your mother, grandmother and your aunt took the child in a car and had her secretly adopted." I wanted to ask him so many questions but was frightened to do so. One main question was running through my mind; did she have the same horrendous upbringing that I had?

That weekend I tried on various occasions to find out more details about the adopted sister but without success. Before I left for home, I asked one more question, "Does she know about me?" "No she doesn't," he replied honestly, "Marie Therese, when we received her letter then a few years later a letter arrived from you, it certainly was a shock to us." How many more are there? I asked myself.

I was now more determined than ever to discover my true identity. The more I heard, the more I wanted and needed to know. I set about trying to find out more about my adopted sister. I even wrote to Sister Elizabeth, asking if she knew about my whole family. In her reply she revealed new information but didn't know about the adopted sister. She did, however, explain that before I had left school, she and the Rev Mother had decided to contact my mother, informing her that I was leaving school and asking if she would like to help me. Apparently my mother had written back frantically, telling the nuns never to contact her again as her son could easily have opened her mail and discovered her secret. Sister Elizabeth ended the letter saying that they didn't write again.

I was stunned by her revelation but more shocked at the response they received from my mother. Was this only part of the story? Why didn't the nuns tell me any of this before I left the orphanage? I also had a feeling that Sister Elizabeth knew more than she had shared with me.

By the end of 1989 I hadn't returned to Donegal, but continued to ask my uncle via letter and phone to let me know where my sister was. On one occasion he responded, "Marie Therese, as far as your sister knows, your mother made one mistake, if she discovers she had made a second one her estimation of your mother wouldn't be too good." I felt like nothing more than a thorn in their side, rather than his sister's daughter who had been hidden away from the whole family!

During that year I received a letter from an old friend called Carol, who had been in the orphanage with me. She said that Sister Elizabeth had given her my address. Carol had traced her family in her mid-20s and went to live with them in South Africa for over 11 years. On the death of her father, the family returned to Ireland. Carol left the orphanage before me and eventually moved to England, so we lost all contact. It was an exciting moment when we met again after 20 years apart. She asked me if I could take her to see the orphanage. I wasn't so enthusiastic but agreed to go with her. I was pretty sure none of the nuns from our time would be there anyway.

A few days later, we headed to the orphanage. We both were completely shocked when the door was answered by Sister Maura! I am sure the expression on our faces said it all. Sister Maura spoke first, "Come in girls you are very welcome." And like little children we followed her to one of the parlours. The same room that we, as children, had scrubbed every week. I could almost smell the disinfectant and wax we used to polish the floors. It brought back horrible memories.

I felt very uncomfortable sitting in front of the nun but thankfully she interrupted my thoughts, "Sister Claire's still here." "Oh really, can we see her please?" I asked hesitantly. "Yes I will go and find her." As soon as she left the room Carol and I looked at each other amazed, "My God, I didn't think she or any of them were still here." "Don't stay long Carol," I warned.

After a few minutes, the two nuns entered the room, linking arms. Sister Maura gently helped Sister Claire into an armchair and proceeded to ask us what we had done with our lives. We spoke for a while and when the conversation dried up, silence took over. I felt intimated and was too afraid to ask many questions. Sister Claire suddenly stared at me before asking in a very weak voice, "Who are you now?" "Marie Rogers," I answered as clearly as I could, realising she was quite deaf. She looked up and asked me the same question again. I repeated myself. "Ah yes," she said, "you're the wee one whose mother had the hotel where we did our collections." I looked at Carol, totally lost for words. Sister Maura interjected quickly, "I think you are tired now Sister, I'll take you back to your room." And with that, they left the room.

"Did you hear that old nun's statement Carol?" I said angrily, "Imagine her knowing about my mother's hotel and me trying to find out who the hell I am. They damn well know plenty about us!" We decided it was time to leave, so made the excuse that we had somewhere else important to be.

As we walked out of the orphanage, we both looked back. I don't know what Carol was thinking but I was relieved to be walking away from it. I hoped never to return. Carol visited me again and revealed how she and her mother didn't get on and that she was moving to England to live with two other girls who had also been in the orphanage. We have remained in contact ever since.

Five years later my determination to find my adopted sister finally paid off. My uncle finally gave in and said he would contact her, letting her know all about me. I didn't care what her reaction might be, another brush off wasn't going to make much difference now. Nevertheless I hoped that she, of all people, might appreciate my urge to become part of a family circle. Sadly, days of waiting for a letter grew into months, then years … and nothing.

Chapter Nine

SHATTERED DREAMS

B Y 1990 I WAS experiencing dreadful back pain. It had
started in the 80s and I had tried strengthening my
back muscles by cycling regularly and playing more
badminton. One evening in 1982, while collecting coal
from the coalbunker, I went to stand up and suddenly
felt an excruciating pain in the lower part of my back and
was completely unable to move. After a few minutes I was
able to stand up and eventually the pain eased. A few
months later I had another episode and thankfully it too
disappeared. Unfortunately, over time the gaps between
the pain became shorter and the pain itself became more
intense. I had many sleepless nights and it got to the stage
that the only way I could even turn over in the bed was
to get up and walk around to the other side of the bed.
Turning and standing became my biggest difficulties.

I didn't mention my back problem to anyone because
once a nurse complains about back pain it often means
the end of their nursing career. However, as time passed

I began to struggle with the physical side of nursing. I felt sure that some kind of darkness was closing in on me but it didn't prepare me for what happened next.

One evening on duty I was simply walking down the ward when I was gripped by a terrible pain in my back. It caused my spine to actually tilt. Another nurse was behind me at the time and seeing me stop so abruptly, she asked "Nurse Rogers; are you alright?" I physically couldn't move with the sharpness of the pain but eventually it eased enough for me to continue my duties.

By now I had mentioned my back to some of my nursing colleagues. They suggested I seek advice from one of the consultants, which I did. After an examination, the consultant said that there may be a disc problem and he would record it but I asked him not to for fear of losing the job I had fought so hard to achieve. Unfortunately, a few weeks later I was admitted to the ward I nursed in. Little did I realise that this was only the start of a very long battle.

After some weeks on bed rest and with traction pulling my spine into place, a myelogram was carried out. I was shocked to discover that I had a large central prolapsed disc of the spine. I always knew there was something quite wrong with my back but I was taken aback by the results all the same. To my relief, it was a problem that could be corrected but unfortunately it wasn't a straightforward textbook case. The pain was so excruciating at times that I required a lot of painkillers.

One Saturday evening I knew by the sensation in my

pelvic region that something terrible was happening to my spine, which had me screaming in pain. The consultant was sent for and in less than half an hour I was rushed to theatre for surgery.

As a nurse I had walked the corridor to surgery daily, bringing worried patients to and from the same theatre that I was being wheeled into. Now I was on the other side of the coin, and it was the most frightening experience.

The surgery lasted a few hours and thankfully I began to improve slightly. I concentrated on getting better so I could get back to my nursing duties and the job I loved. However, shortly before my discharge I experienced my first psychological knock. The consultant came to speak to me during his ward round. He was compassionate but frank, "It's time for a career change Marie. The surgery was very extensive and your back isn't good therefore you will have to forget about nursing again." I heard what he said in slow motion. "I can work in the children's unit," I answered quickly, although I knew realistically that working with children was even more physically demanding.

After he left the room Sister Lynn sat on the bed and did her best to reassure and console me. I don't think I heard a word she said. I just couldn't believe that the job I had worked so hard to get was about to be taken from me. Why had I struggled with my studies for nothing? Was I going to lose all the nursing friends I had made? Was I going to be socially isolated with no employment or future? All these questions raced through my mind and unfortunately were only a taste of what was to come.

Following the surgery I had a plaster cast put on to keep my spine stable while it was healing. I was sent home from hospital but after a few months was readmitted with severe pain. I couldn't put my finger on what was causing the pain but I knew that something really wasn't right. I vaguely remembered something happening to me as I was lifted from the theatre trolley after my operation. I felt a painful click but was still groggy from the anaesthetic and couldn't remember it clearly.

My first back surgery took place in February 1990 but it continued to deteriorate. In September of that year I was flown to England for a MRI scan, which showed another bulging disc. I was told I needed another operation and became quite depressed about the whole thing. Between the surgery and losing a brilliant career, I was just miserable. I had my second surgery and returned home but my recovery was short lived.

In June 1991, I was seen by three different consultants who decided I needed a metal rod inserted into my spine to stabilise it. I was more nervous this time and it turned out with good reason. I didn't come round from my operation until a week later. By this stage I was in the Intensive Care Unit of another hospital, where I had been fighting for my life on a life support machine. You hear all the time about people close to death who travel down a dark tunnel and see a light at the end of it, but my experience wasn't like that at all. I do remember feeling like I was going down a dark tunnel but there was no light. I was simply fighting for all my worth until suddenly there an almighty clap from somewhere. That was the last sound I heard until a voice spoke from above. No, I hadn't entered Heaven!

In spite of being extremely ill and on a ventilator, my brain was active. I wanted to ask questions but couldn't and my body felt locked in, with no ability to function. It was terrifying. Fortunately I improved and on the day I was being transferred to the hospital where I had the surgery, a doctor explained that I had tried desperately to say something when I woke up. She showed me a clipboard on which I had scrawled the words "Am I dying?" in childish handwriting. I was amazed at this disclosure.

My nursing friends didn't forget me. They took turns to sit with me morning, noon and night during my time in the Intensive Care Unit. My friend Jenny later told me that while sitting with me, a nun had appeared, all in black and began praying over me. Jenny froze, thinking, God Almighty, if she wakes up and sees this nun standing over her, she'll either think she's in Heaven or back in the orphanage!

As the drugs started to leave my system I felt horrendous; talk about 'cold turkey!' I experienced terrible hallucinations such as giants being beaten up the walls of my room by a group of dwarfs! I was taken for an x-ray the day after I returned from the Intensive Care Unit. While

I waited, the radiographer told me not to move. I was so weak that I couldn't move much anyway so I didn't think much of what he said until I returned to the ward. The surgeon came in and announced that he was happy with the x-ray. My heart leapt. However, he also explained that I had lost a lot of blood during surgery, which is why I went to Intensive Care. There was another problem.

During my surgery, a large needle had been accidentally left in my spine. It needed to be removed immediately. I thought I was hearing things but after the consultant left the room Sister Lynn showed me the x-ray. It was terrifying just how close the needle was to my spine.

The doctor performed the surgery himself the following morning and thankfully it went quite well. However all the surgery left me suffering from chronic back pain and prevented me from walking any distance. My hard-earned freedom had suddenly been snatched away from me and I asked myself was I being punished for leaving Tommy and Jean in their later years? I really had no idea how I was going to cope with this change in my life.

In 1991 I received a phone call that would top it all. "Hello Marie Therese, how are you? Are you sitting down?" my uncle asked. I sensed by the tone of his voice that something was amiss, "I'm sorry to have to tell you, that your mother died last night in Letterkenny Hospital." There was silence for a few seconds before I finally asked, "What's happening about her funeral?" If I had wanted to attend, what he said next ensured I wouldn't, "It would be

best if you don't come but you could send a nice wreath."
To be honest I couldn't have gone to her funeral anyway
as I really wasn't physically strong enough to travel. I sat
back remembering my time at the fair in Donegal and
how the two women had thought I resembled somebody.

After the phone call, I sat and cried. I was crying for
something I didn't have yet always wanted, a mother,
and now she was gone, taking with her hundreds of
unanswered questions. As I stood looking out at the
dreary day that suited the dismal news I had just received,
I thought of the only time I had met my mother. I had
a haunting memory of her frail skeleton, sitting in an
armchair in the middle of the psycho-geriatric ward in
Letterkenny. That impression will be forever imprinted in
my mind.

I did as was suggested and sent a wreath, writing on the
little card attached, "From your Daughter Marie Therese."
I had two choices: I could either let myself go downhill
mentally and physically, as before my breakdown, or I
could pick myself up and make the most of what life had
to offer. Thankfully I chose the latter.

In 1993 a consultant suggested a new procedure that
could help my chronic back pain. Naturally I jumped
at any chance to ease my pain, even though it would be
expensive at £5000. Unfortunately the procedure was not
only painful but unsuccessful and the electronic stimulator
that was inserted had to be removed six months later.

The following year, another consultant offered me

another procedure, which I went for. It involved injecting a drug that he hoped would help the pain. The procedure was carried out at the hospital I had all my surgery in and while I was lying groggy in the recovery bay, a nurse asked for Donna Marie's phone number. Donna Marie was Jean's sister. The next morning Sister Lynn came into my room, closed the door and sat down on the side of my bed, "Marie Therese while you were in theatre yesterday, we were contacted by the police who were looking for Jean's sister." I was confused by her comment until I remembered mumbling Donna Marie's number to a nurse. "Why did the police want her number?" I asked puzzled. "The police were called to Jean's house after the RSPCA couldn't gain access. She was found dead by the police sitting in her chair," Sister Lynn explained softly. I eased myself back on the pillow and gave a sigh of relief.

I hadn't the same sorrow for Jean's death that I had for Tommy's. I left the hospital that evening and a few days later attended her funeral. My friend Helen came with me for support. My final duty needed to be carried out and I also needed to convince myself that she was definitely dead. Only then would I finally be free and have peace of mind.

I made my way to a pew at the back of the Chapel but my friend Helen whispered, "Come on up to the front Marie, you have nothing to fear now." I could see members of her family ahead of me and was afraid they would lash out at me for leaving Tommy and Jean. I sat at one side of the

Chapel and the family sat at the other. Donna Marie crossed the aisle to where I was sitting, took hold of my hand and sympathised with me, before slowly walking away.

As I made my way up the aisle to receive Holy Communion and neared Jean's coffin, I had a horrifying flashback. One evening, when I was nine years old, we all had to go to the darkened Chapel to receive Holy Communion. At the top of the aisle was the coffin of a child called Susan. I whispered to one of my wee friends, "Why is Susan sleeping in that box?" Apparently poor Susan had been taken out for a holiday by a family and had somehow gone missing in the snow. Her frozen body was found some days later. My thoughts were interrupted by Helen asking, "Marie, are you alright?" She took me gently by the arm and lead me forwards to receive communion. "You are absolutely freezing," she commented but I just followed her without uttering a word.

As the coffin was being carried out of the Chapel at the end of the Funeral Mass, I asked Helen, "Is she really in there?" "Oh she is definitely in there without a doubt Marie," she confirmed. I was so mixed up in my mind that I didn't know if the coffin held Susan or Jean. As I left the Chapel I had the most uncanny feeling that if I looked over my shoulder Jean would be standing behind me, arms crossed and watching my every move. I chose not to attend the graveside, having had such a strange experience when Tommy died.

It was months before it finally sunk in that Jean really

was gone for good. It was only then that I could close that chapter of my life and move on. A few months later, Donna Marie contacted me to say that while clearing out Jean's house she had found a little Tyrone crystal basket lying with some old items ready for the bin. I called to her house for it some weeks later and was pleased to see my little gift from the staff in the Cardiac Ward again.

In 1992 I was allocated a social worker called Barbara by my GP. I really don't know how I would have managed without her. During that year Barbara suggested I attend a Day Centre for people with physical disabilities a few times a week.

In the end Barbara was the first person to hear my full story and really seemed to understand the despair I was experiencing. She gave me confidence and helped me discover that there was more to life than nursing. Most importantly, she gave me hope.

Time passed and I lost interest in the Day Centre. I discussed this with Barbara, explaining how I felt like I was wasting my life away. During our conversation, she said, "Marie you should write down your emotions and feelings." Jenny had suggested the same thing a few years earlier. I decided it was worth working towards but my English grammar wasn't so good, so I applied to study a correspondence course in English Language. Would I achieve a better grade than the one I got in 1972? That was the start of my studies and the beginning of a story that I hoped would some day be read.

In the late 1990s, Barbara contacted an organisation called the Cedar Foundation. This organisation provided services to children and adults with disabilities, including youth, educational and independent living support. With their help I was able to obtain various typing qualifications and in 2000 they offered me a part-time job, which I accepted. I ended up working for the Cedar Foundation in Belfast for 10 years. I loved every minute of it. Sister Lynn had once said to me that there was more to life than nursing and I was now realising that she was right.

Chapter Ten

IN SEARCH OF ANSWERS

URING THE SUMMER OF 1995, Barbara made
arrangements for me to have a short holiday at the
Share Centre, a huge complex in Fermanagh catering for
both able and disabled people. The centre was supported
by professional people who worked voluntarily, helping
with cooking and organising various activities for the
clients each week.

The weather was beautiful that summer and I had a
wonderful break but on one of the nights I couldn't sleep,
as I was having a lot of pain in my back. I sat up in the
sitting room and chatted to one of the summer volunteers,
a social worker called Jack. As we talked I told him a little
about my story. To my surprise, Jack told me that he had
a friend who lived just 3 miles from my mother's hotel.
His friend was a local historian who knew all there was to
know about the locals, past and present. I couldn't believe
my luck. Jack said he would contact his friend and be in
touch but warned he may not get back to me for some

time. I didn't care, what were a few months when I'd waited 45 years?!

Five months later Jack phoned me as promised and I made arrangements to meet his historian friend. My friend Bernie offered to travel with me. She and I worked together and often travelled to and from work. I remember asking her on the way home one day, "Bernie, who are you like, your Mum or Dad?" She gave me a strange look before responding, "My goodness why are you asking that Marie?" "No particular reason," I answered.

Bernie took a day off work and we headed for Dunkineely, in Donegal. We discovered that Dunkineely is only one street and that the historian owned and lived in a little pub at the end of it. The area is quite popular with tourists, who often visit his pub to quench their thirsts and listen to Irish music before continuing on their journey around the beautiful Donegal coasts.

We arrived early in the afternoon and sat in the car for a few minutes watching people coming and going but few entered the pub. After a few minutes Bernie got my wheelchair out and we made our way towards the tiny pub door. A short, slim, elderly man wearing a familiar Irish cap answered the door. "Eh, my name is Marie Therese Rogers; I spoke to you on the phone last week," I said nervously. "Come in dear," he said, opening the door wider for the wheelchair. He led us into a small, old fashioned bar, furnished with dark chairs and stools, and with an open fire taking centre stage. The walls were covered with old pictures of Donegal and its people, and although it was in need of a lick of paint, it was very warm and inviting.

As we settled ourselves, he launched straight in with a question, "You're the baby born in the forties aren't you?" I sat back in my chair, feeling a little uncomfortable beneath his gaze. "No, I was born in 1950," I answered, but knew what he was getting at. "Are you sure you weren't born in the forties?" he asked. "Definitely not," I said confidently, taking my birth certificate and other documents from my handbag. "Well now, Dinnie had many a drink in here with Josie," he announced, looking through my documents, "Sure the whole area knew that Josie and Dinnie had a wee one, but nobody mentioned it and as far as I know the baby was taken away." I looked at Bernie, not quite believing that this man had actually met my father.

Even though he had seen my birth certificate, the historian asked my date of birth again. He still wasn't convinced I was born in 1950 and looked confused by this information. "Your father was very fond of your mother." he said. "What was he like as a person?" I asked hungrily. "Ach sure didn't they both frequent the pub many a time and fine people, they were." I noticed he spoke in past tense as though both were dead. "Imagine; you're not the baby born in the forties, well, well. You certainly were a secret," he muttered, as thought in deep thought.

I told the historian my story to date, including how I

knew about my sister but hadn't been in contact with her as yet. He sat back in his chair and listened intently, before commenting, "I don't think there is a person in this area who knew about you but the whole of the Glenties knew about the other baby, dear me."

"You look like your mother and also some of your cousins down the street in the shop," he told me, "You should call and see them before you go home." I was delighted with all this new information and was glad Bernie was with me in case I forgot something. He told me the names of my cousins and I was taken aback because the surname was the same as the solicitor who visited me in the factory. What was the connection? I thought. He also told me that my father was a Tipperary man and had worked as an engineer.

All too soon, it was time to end our informative meeting with the historian but before we left his cosy pub, he announced that an old lady who had worked for my mother at the hotel was still around. He left the room briefly and returned with the old lady's name, address and phone number. I certainly didn't expect to hear all this.

Bernie and I decided not to call on the cousins without prior warning but set off home discussing everything we had just heard. I was overjoyed with all this new information and the following morning I dialled the number for the old lady. After a few seconds, a loud but friendly voice answered the phone.

I briefly explained who I was and about the meeting

with the historian. "Oh yes, I surely know the man. Your father was a wonderful man, in and out of the hotel every day he was." I didn't have a chance to respond before the lady continued on, "He was a Tipperary man and worked for many months on the harbour pier, you know." She spoke as though it was common knowledge and I should have known. She rambled on for some time, reminding me a little of Mrs Hogan, the lady in the hospital in Letterkenny, but it was all music to my ears.

She asked me a few questions and when I told her the year I was born, I sensed she was as confused as the historian, "Oh, are you sure you weren't born in the forties?" I didn't respond directly, so she continued on talking.

My face was wet with tears as I listened to this old lady talk for Ireland. She was quite happy to tell me anything she could. She told me that she had kept an old photograph of the staff she had worked with in the hotel and that my father was also in the picture. "Oh my God, will you please let me have it?" I asked, overwhelmed with excitement, "I will copy the photograph and get your one back to you as soon as possible." "As soon as I find the picture of your father I will send it to you immediately," she replied. I was going to see what my father actually looked like!

About three weeks later I had my first glimpse of my father. The photograph was tiny and he was standing behind a group of people. I wanted show my friends and tell them, "This is my father!" Tear drops landed on the picture, just as they had on my mother's photograph in the factory all those years ago. I stared at this stranger who was part of my birth and desperately wanted to know what he was like as a person. I was pleased that I had heard only kind comments about him in the past few months.

I contacted a local Tipperary radio station about my story, hoping some locals would hear me and know something about my father. It was suggested by the radio station that I also contact the parishes in the area, which I did. To my delight, in 1997 a parish priest wrote to me, telling me that my father had lived in Cloughjordan and had worked in Donegal around the time of my birth. He also revealed that he was a single man in the early 50s, later moving to England where he got married. He asked if I knew that my father had a bit of a drink problem and that he died in 1981? This disclosure saddened me greatly.

The priest also mentioned that he had contacted my father's niece and she in turn contacted Mrs Moloney in England, but nothing came from it. I later found out that the same niece was in fact a religious nun but was delighted to discover she wasn't of the same order that I was with as a child!

Regrettably that was the last contact I had with the priest from Tipperary. I rang a few times, hungry for more answers but was dismissed with comments like, "Och sure that was a long time ago and should be forgotten." I was once again left with the tiny photograph of a man who appeared to be liked by most but never knew the child he helped produce. At least I had some answers.

In 1996 I received a letter from my uncle and inside his letter was another envelope with a postmark from England. My persistence had paid off; the letter was from the adopted sister I wanted to know. In my excitement I could barely open the envelope. I skimmed over the pages, looking for information about her search but she mostly wrote about her own family and adoptive mother, who she seemed close to. This closeness saddened me, not that I wasn't pleased for her but it made me think, if only I had being given the same chance.

She mentioned how, following the death of her father, she had gone in search of her biological mother but couldn't take it upon herself to see her. I imagine it hadn't been easy for her when she was told that she had been adopted. I was struck by one comment that she made at the start of her letter, "To think that I grew up an only child." When I got to the end of the letter there was no surname. I sensed that her family didn't know about me and her letter didn't give me any answers. I was slightly disappointed but still excited that contact had been made.

Having obtained her address from my uncle, I replied, hoping it would be the start of two sisters getting to know each other. So many questions ran through my mind: Did she know her father? Did she ever meet him? How and when did she make contact with my uncle? Although I kept in touch with all my half-sisters, I had accepted that I would never get any answers from them. I also understood that my brother would probably never know that I even existed. I hoped that my sister in England might be the one to fill the gap in my life regarding my roots.

By 1995 I was well into the writing of my story although it was just in essay form at this stage. I was keen to know when my mother's husband had died and if there had been a will, so I requested his will through the Births, Deaths and Marriages in the South of Ireland. A copy of his Will arrived many weeks later and what I read completely blew me away. I quote, "Should my wife remarry after my death I direct that her interest in my said property shall cease and become void." I actually felt sorry for my mother at this point, realising that she was completely tied. Again I had gained information yet wanted to learn even more. I was more determined than ever to continue my search.

With Sister Elizabeth getting much older I was determined to keep quizzing her before it was too late. I wrote to her and asked about the green dress I had received. There is an old saying, those who wait the longest are the best rewarded, but what she said made me sick to the core, "The green dress was actually sent by your mother but when other children asked where the dress came from the Rev Mother ordered it be removed and it was suggested that your mother send money but what became of that I don't know."

Her revelation was an eye-opener and it made me very

angry. Imagine, I thought it was the teacher from the special school that had bought me the beautiful green dress. Now I understood why Sister Elizabeth had fussed so much that day just for a teacher to visit. I realised the only way to get closure to this whole saga was to return to the orphanage and speak directly to the nun currently in charge. When I phoned the orphanage the nun who answered said, "There really isn't much point in you calling as I don't know if I can give you any answers." She certainly wasn't going to put me off.

I asked Barbara to accompany me to the orphanage and on a lovely bright spring day in May in 1996, she collected me. As she drove into the large grounds, it was as if time had stood still. I had a flashback as we got out of the car. I could see myself and many of my friends perched on the climber looking over the huge wall, watching birds fly overhead and wishing we could fly to freedom like them. The sound of children laughing filled my ears until Barbara's voice interrupted my thoughts, "Are you coming Marie?" "Where are the swings; climbers and children?" I whispered, suddenly realising the playground was empty. I looked up at the huge wall topped with glass and barbed wire, and realised it was not as menacing to me now as an adult.

The building was no longer for orphans but was now for the care of the elderly. The door was opened by one of the older girls I remembered from my childhood. She must have never left the place. She led us down the same hallway Carol and I had walked along a few years earlier; but now the stone floor we had scrubbed every week was hidden by fancy carpet.

We were escorted into the same parlour Carol and I had sat in and told that Rev Mother would be in shortly. I looked around the room and could almost smell the wax and polish I had used to clean it. "We only entered these parlours to scrub and wax them," I whispered to Barbara as we waited. We chatted quietly for a few minutes until we heard footsteps approaching the door. I shivered slightly and Barbara, sensing my fear, placed her hand on mine before taking a seat opposite me. "You'll be fine," she whispered.

A tall nun entered the room and shook our hands before declaring, "Oh I am not staying." I looked up at her and thought to myself, God I don't recognise this person at all. As if reading my thoughts, she continued, "It is Mother Sarah who remembers you, not me, so you can put your questions to her." At that she turned on her heels and left.

Mother Sarah entered the room. I expected to be looking up at her but was now looking down at a very small, pale, old woman with sharp features. I tried to introduce Barbara but Mother Sarah talked over me, as if she hadn't heard me. She directed her conversation to Barbara, "Oh yes I remember you well Marie, you were a junior and a very quiet child. What can I do for you?" Staring at her but without making eye contact, I said, "I don't remember you that well." "Och, sure you were in Sister Elizabeth's class," she interrupted again and I realised she was reminding me of my educational background. I wanted to shout at her and tell her I wasn't a terrified nine year old anymore. I wanted her to know the kind of person I had become. Thankfully Barbara sensed my disgust and butted in quickly, "Marie, show her your mother's photograph and tell her how you became a nurse."

I spoke with a shaky voice, as though afraid of repercussions, "I became a nurse." "My goodness, did you do nursing?" she asked still looking at Barbara as if it was only the two of them in the room. I handed her my nursing certificates and the photograph of my mother. She took a fleeting glimpse at both without even touching them, turned to Barbara and asked, "Did she qualify?" I was mortified, as much for Barbara as for myself. It didn't really matter what I said, this nun wasn't interested and it showed. Not once during the meeting did she say, "Oh well done Marie, I am delighted you did well."

Our uncomfortable conversation continued until I announced, "I would like to see any records held about me." I was actually mid-sentence when she interrupted again, "Goodness me, we don't have that stuff." I repeated the question several times, knowing it was annoying her, and eventually she gave in, "I don't know what you want to know, but I will go and see if there is any information." As she left, I called out after her, "Please bring the reference book back with you."

"God she is so intimidating Barbara," I said after she

was out of sight. I knew she couldn't do me any harm anymore but I still wanted out of the place. She returned after a few minutes, with the older girl carrying a tray of tea and biscuits behind her. I looked at the girl sadly and felt so sorry that she was living in a building with so many dreadful memories.

Mother Sarah handed me a tiny piece of paper that had been torn off the corner of a larger sheet, declaring, "This is all I have." I looked at the scribbled piece of paper, showing my date of birth, the day I entered and the day I left the institution, and nothing more. I stared at the nun indignantly, "Sure I know this information and anyway my surname doesn't have a D in it." I was so furious that I wanted to rip the paper into tiny pieces and throw them back at her, but I kept my composure.

The atmosphere was very tense so I changed the subject. We were getting nowhere this way. "Have you seen any of the other girls?" I asked. "Indeed I have," she replied smugly, "and that girl, oh yes Colette, imagine her coming for my help to find her mother! I told her she was better off without her but of course she insisted and discovered her mother was poor." My blood was boiling, "Everybody has the God given right to know who they are and their identity. Nobody should deny them of that right." Her only answer was, "We were good to you girls; we did our best."

Our meeting was brought to an end and on our way out Barbara pushed my wheelchair towards her car. "I must see how you manage to get the wheelchair into the car," Mother Sarah said. "You don't need to watch," I replied coldly but she ignored me and continued to follow us. As Barbara was putting the wheelchair into the boot of the car, I could see in the wing mirror that the nun was talking to her. Barbara told me that the Sister had asked, "Don't you know that Marie's a slow learner?" To which Barbara had replied, "Yes I am quite aware of that but don't you ever forget what the slow learner has done and without your help!" Barbara was furious but I really wasn't surprised. I actually felt sad that after 30 years, the only thing this nun still believed was that I was a slow learner.

In the late 1990s I had an urge to visit my mother's grave and Bernie happily agreed to travel to Donegal with me. We had become great friends and she often invited me to spend weekends with her and her family. Strangely enough, when I first met Bernie's parents I remember commenting, "Yes you're so like your Dad." "You asked me that one time coming home from work," she answered laughing.

When we arrived at the graveyard, just like my experience with Tommy, we couldn't find my mother's grave. However, I was amazed at the amount of Rogers that had been buried there. After some searching we eventually found it and Bernie helped me to the site. While standing looking down at my mother's resting place I felt so, so empty and lost. It was as if a terrible black cloud had descended from above that was trying to choke me. "I should put a little plant here Bernie. Her grave needs some kind of life," I whispered sadly.

Bernie went off to find a plant and I sat on a little wall and gathered my thoughts. "You never give me the answers I needed and have finally taken them to the next world," I whimpered to her grave, choking back the tears. Thankfully the graveyard was empty so no one heard me.

Bernie returned with a little hardy plant and helped me down onto my knees. I dug a small hole in and placed the plant deeply into the damp soil, making sure it was going to stay there. "Come on Marie, let's go home," Bernie said softly after a while, easing me away from the grave. She noticed I was clenching something tightly in my hand and asked, "What's that Marie?" I opened my hand to reveal the two photographs of my mother and father, now rather crumpled.

We had to pass the graveyard to get to the main road and while driving past I glanced back thinking how sad it was that the person who brought me into this world had now left it and that I never had the chance to know her. It was perhaps even sadder that I would never have a chance to visit my father's grave, as he must be buried in England.

In the late 90s I was interviewed by the *Belfast Telegraph* after a friend contacted them about me writing a book. An article appeared in the paper the following week and a few days after that the editor rang me to say that somebody had contacted them regarding the article and wanted to speak to me. I couldn't believe it and was so excited! The editor passed my details on and a few days later a lady rang saying that she was a retired midwife who had worked in Lisieux Nursing Home in the early 50s. She remembered my mother well, "Your mother was a very attractive woman and extremely wealthy." She said that every weekend my father visited the nursing home, right up to the time of my birth. I was completely spellbound by what she was telling me. "I and my colleagues heard your mother say she would be back for the baby, but we felt otherwise. Your father loved that woman and I think would have married her."

She clarified that my Godmother owned the nursing home and how she sadly died in the 70s. Before ending she got me a contact for my Godmother's daughter. Some weeks later we met up for coffee, where she filled me in on what the nursing home was like and gave me a photograph of it. She also put me in touch with two of my Godmother's sisters-in-laws. They said that they often wondered how my Godmother knew my mother. Now they understood and they also revealed that she visited my mother's hotel many times over the years.

Chapter Eleven

THE FINAL JOURNEY

IN 2009 I VISITED St Patrick's Chapel in Donegall Street which is just across the road from where the Private Nursing Home was located and was the place where I was baptised. The Priest was very kind that day and allowed me to look at the large ledger showing baptismal information. I couldn't believe my eyes when I read that my father was actually present at my baptism and had to pay a sum of money because he wasn't married. It was the priest who said, "Do you see your name in the column showing the child's name?" I looked at it and saw that the name written was "Marie Therese Moloney". In another column something had been rubbed out, as though somebody had tried to erase it. The priest and I examined it for a while and realised that it was my mother's name that somebody had tried to scrape off the ledger. It was around this time that I decided I would search the world until I found my father and I didn't care how long it took.

That year I felt that I needed a good holiday and

knew that Bernie was going to visit her sister Brenda in Tipperary. I decided to join her, hoping I might discover something new about my father while I was there, but I didn't mention this to Bernie. I also contacted my cousins on my mother's side and suggested we meet. It had been a long time since I had seen some of my cousins and some I had never even met. They offered to get together in a hotel in Bray. I asked Bernie if she would like to travel to Bray with me, then we could travel on to Tipperary from there. She readily agreed.

At the end of August 2009, Bernie and I set off on a holiday that would never be forgotten. The journey was lovely and we stopped off a few times for coffee and lunch, before arriving at the hotel in Bray where I was meeting my cousins that evening. Once settled into the room, we had a rest before the get together. I was nervous about seeing some of my cousins for the first time, even though I knew quite a bit about them from my aunt and uncle. At least I wasn't as worried as the day that I met my aunt and uncle in the hotel in Derry.

When we arrived in the lounge, there was nobody about but thankfully we only had to wait a few minutes. My elderly aunt entered, accompanied by her two sons and two of her daughters. The eldest son Hugh had brought his wife Mary and their 8 year old grandchild David. He had arranged to stay in a hotel nearby because the hotel I was staying in was fully booked. He explained he was staying a few days as he was determined to spend as much time with me as possible. I got on extremely well with Hugh and Mary, and really enjoyed their company.

When all the cousins arrived, we had a meal in the hotel restaurant. Throughout the dinner, some of the cousins asked more questions than others. They were mostly interested in my time in the orphanage but I didn't feel uncomfortable telling them about it. I was so busy answering their questions that I didn't ask them many myself.

Following dinner, photos were taken and we all headed off to Inniskerry, to visit a beautiful stately home called Powerscourt. The gardens were wonderful and we spent hours strolling around them, talking and imagining how the Victorians once lived there in all its grandeur. It was quite late when we got back to the hotel and some of the cousins said their goodbyes. Hugh, Mary, David, Bernie and I settled in the lounge, took further photos and chatted for hours. Hugh and Mary seemed genuinely interest in what I had to say, so I told them about the book I was writing before we parted.

On Tuesday 1 September, we left the hotel and set off for Tipperary. Before we left Belfast, I had gathered up all the information I had about both my parents and brought it with me. I even had my father's works documents from the company who employed him at the harbour in Killybegs, Donegal. I hoped Brenda lived somewhere close to Cloughjordan and Emill, where my father came from but I didn't mention any of this to Bernie. I really wasn't sure if anything would come of the trip and was just going to play it by ear.

It was very late when we arrived at Brenda's house in Templemore. We settled down to a warm dinner and a well-earned rest. Bernie decided to have an early night but I was too excited to settle, so Brenda, her husband Stephen and I sat up until the wee hours of the morning talking. Brenda knew very little about my background and my story upset her. I wanted to keep things upbeat so told her about how I was tracing my roots. I didn't mention the documents I had tucked away in my handbag. To my delight she said that Cloughjordan was just a few miles from her. I was overjoyed.

The following day, we all had breakfast together and around 11.00 am Brenda suggested we head off to Cloughjordan. Although there wasn't much sun, it was a lovely warm day. I was so excited I doubt I would have cared if it was snowing. I had this strange feeling that something was going to happen, maybe not that day but before the holiday was over. Maybe it was because I had Bernie with me. She had been with me through so much, meeting the historian in Dunkineely, visiting my mother's grave and also my cousins at the hotel in Bray. I wondered if she brought me good luck and hoped she would here in Tipperary.

We had been driving for about 15 minutes when I noticed a sign for Cloughjordan. "Brenda, there's Cloughjordan!" I shouted like an excited child. When we arrived in the little town I looked around hungrily. It appeared to be just one long street, which Brenda drove down very slowly to allow me time to take everything in. Upon seeing a chemist, Bernie asked Brenda to stop. The town was very quiet and as we waited for Bernie, nobody passed us, not even to go into the little shop. It was like a ghost town, standing still to allow me to see as much as possible. It was quite eerie.

Brenda interrupted my observation, "Do you see that pub over there Marie Therese?" She was pointing to a pub called The Clough Inn. "I sure do," I replied. "Why don't we go there for our lunch?" she suggested, giving me a sly grin. I wonder if she knows what I'm up to, I thought. The pub was quite near to the pavement, with no steps, which meant Brenda could drive the car right up to the door. We could see that the wheelchair wouldn't fit through the narrow doorway but I was able to sit in a seat near the door.

It was quite an old pub, full of little alcoves to give people privacy. There were only three or four people in the place; three men drinking and a young girl behind the counter, so all heads turned towards us when we entered. They obviously knew we were visitors. We sat a few minutes before the young girl asked if we wanted a drink. We ordered tea and biscuits then Bernie went outside for a few minutes.

I glanced down at my handbag, making sure nobody could see the documents it contained. Bernie returned but instead of joining her sister and I, she went up to the main bar and began a conversation with the locals. "Is there anybody called Moloney around here?" I heard her ask. I put my hand on Brenda's and whispered "What is she up to, did you hear that?" All three men answered simultaneously, "Ah sure is it Dinnie you're looking for?" "My God, Brenda, did you hear that?" I asked. "I can get his number from my daddy," the girl called from behind the counter. At the same time a man took his mobile phone out and started talking to somebody. I was doing my best to eavesdrop and was beside myself with excitement.

The man got up and walked towards us, still talking to the person on his mobile. To my amazement, he handed me the phone, "Here ye are you can have a chat to Denis." Here I was, in a pub full of complete strangers, about to speak to a man called Denis Moloney! My excitement was replaced with fear and confusion, I thought my father was dead. Did the priest tell me wrong? The voice at the end of the phone sounded too young to be my father, "Are you down for the wedding from Belfast? "No, no," I replied, my voice quivering, "I am actually doing a genealogy research into the name Moloney and it so happens, my name is Moloney." "Really and how do you spell it?" My God, I thought, hoping I spelt it the same way. He didn't say whether I had or not.

"How can I help you, do you need some questions answered?" he asked. "Well, I suppose that would be good," I replied, thinking you're very right, I need many questions answered. "Where are you? You can come up here but the place isn't too clean," he continued. "Well, that would be fine," I replied, my hand shaking as I handed the phone back to the local man. He walked out of the pub still chatting away to this Denis Moloney. "Bernie, he's going to catch on what we are at," I whispered. "You did well Marie Therese, I wouldn't even have thought of what to say," Brenda reassured me. "I can't believe that I have just spoken to a Denis Moloney, somebody with exactly the same name as my father," I stuttered, "My God, what do we do now?" Before either of my friends had a chance to respond, the man came back into the pub and said, "Come on, you can follow me to Denis's house. He's happy to answer any questions you have."

I was shaking as we got into the car, "Oh my God, what am I going to say girls?" I was overwhelmed with the prospect of meeting someone that may have know my father. I was also terrified that he wouldn't know anything about him at all.

We followed the local man for about 10 minutes until he stopped at an old style farmhouse with a glass porch at the front. "He said the place wasn't tidy," I told the sisters, thinking it looked very neat and tidy from the outside. "Don't be worrying Marie, you'll be fine, we will just play it by ear and if it turns out well that'll be a bonus and if not we'll move to the next plan," Bernie said confidently.

I glanced up at the house, which was positioned slightly above ground level, and saw a man coming to the door.

"Merciful God, what'll I say?" I spluttered but my friends had already gotten out of the car. A tall, well-dressed man opened the front door and made his way over to the car. "Come in, come in, you're very welcome," he said in a strong Tipperary accent, with his hand held out, ready to greet us. I nudged the sisters in front of me, terrified the man might recognise my father in me. Bernie looked over her shoulder at me and whispered, "You're a Moloney!"

Denis took hold of my hand, supported my arm and directed me up a low step into his home, before guiding me towards an armchair beside a stove. After settling into the seat I noticed how warm and inviting the house was. Everything was well kept and tidy in the kitchen we were sitting in. He must have got mixed up when he said the place wasn't tidy, I thought.

"Now how can I help you?" he asked, looking at each of us in turn. For a few seconds nobody spoke, then the sisters glanced over at me. "And you're not at the wedding?" Denis asked, interrupting the awkward silence. "Eh no," I said quietly, "I am doing genealogy research and have focused on a few names and one of those names happens to be a Denis Moloney. We popped into a pub today for lunch and got chatting to some locals and you know the rest." I looked straight at him, hoping I had convinced him and also searching his face for any likeness to the tiny photograph I had of my father.

Meanwhile the local man who had brought us to the house was hovering behind us, listening to the whole conversation. It was making me quite self-conscious and I was careful not to say too much. "This lady lives in Templemore," I said, pointing at Brenda. Denis turned his attention to her and started talking about local issues, which broke the ice.

As the conversation went on I began to feel more comfortable and even had a strange feeling that I was connected to this man somehow. "Sure you'll have a cup of tea," he said, declining Bernie's offer to help. "How far have you got with the names?" he asked, looking straight at me. Distracted by the other conversation and tea, I almost forgot about the genealogy side of things. "Well, the person I focused on is a Denis Moloney from somewhere around here. I know that this man worked for some years in Donegal as an engineer and later worked and lived in England." "By God, you have plenty of information; that's for sure," he remarked as he handed out the biscuits. I blabbered on about the other false names I was using for the research to throw him off the scent and the conversation continued on to where we were all from.

We were talking for over an hour when I looked at Bernie, hinting that she should go out for a smoke and take the local man from the pub with her. Thankfully Bernie understood and looked at the local as she announced, "I'm going out for a smoke." But before she got up, Denis said quickly, "Ah sure you'll have a smoke in here." She shook her head, "I don't smoke in my own home and won't smoke in anybody else's." "I have none on me," announced the local. "I'll give you one; come on," Bernie replied and they both went outside.

My heart was thumping as I watched them leave the room. What will this man's reaction be when he hears the full story? I thought, clutching my cup of tea tightly. I looked at Brenda and she stood up, walked to the door and closed it tightly before sitting down again. She looked at me as though to say, go for it.

I must have taken the deepest breath of my life before telling Denis the following, "Denis, I have told you the truth about doing research into the name Moloney and it was true that I was specially focusing on Denis Moloney. Isn't your father called Peter?" "Yes that's right," he said. "Didn't your father have a brother called Denis?" I continued. "He did so," he agreed, standing back and looking at me with a puzzled expression. "Denis, the reason I am asking you all these questions is because I had to be sure I had the right person," I explained. Bernie came back into the room alone and I opened my handbag and took out the documents I had been carrying. "I am Denis Moloney's daughter, your uncle's child," I announced, handing him the documents shakily. Denis looked through the documents and then closed them over.

I was terrified of what his reaction would be and I certainly wasn't prepared for what this stranger did next. He walked across the kitchen with his arm outstretched took my hand in his and said very softly, "Well, well, you are very welcome into the family." I burst into tears.

"My God, the local will come back in," I mumbled, embarrassed by my tears. "Ouch sure we'll get rid of him," Denis said and we all laughed. The local came back in and announced he must be going. Before he even had even finished his sentence, Denis answered, "Sure now, that's fine I'll see you soon."

"I am so delighted to hear this news," Denis said genuinely, as I got the tissues out. I looked at Bernie and Brenda and saw they were both crying too. Denis came over to me and put his arm around my back saying, "Come on your hard work is over." I was just so relieved that this man had believed me.

Denis now took the time to look through the other papers and said he was amazed by the amount of information I already had. Upon reading my father's birth certificate, he said, "My goodness, why didn't you show me this first, I would have known immediately you had the right person?" "Oh my God, I had to be so careful and sure that I was on the right track. I didn't want to step on anybody's toes or hurt them. I also didn't know what your reaction would be on hearing this news," I explained.

He said he vaguely remembered hearing something, way back when he was a young boy, about a kind of secret regarding my uncle, but he never heard anything after that. The sisters and I looked at each other and I felt as if a heavy burden had just been lifted from my shoulders. For the first time in nearly 60 years I felt I could relax. Had my search really ended?

"Damn it, this requires a celebration," Denis declared, jumping up and rushing from one cupboard to another, looking for china cups. He put the kettle on and suddenly yelled, "My God, I must get Nora!" He lifted the phone, dialled a number and said excitedly, "Nora, I have a lovely lady here from Belfast." She said something and he replied, "No but I'll tell you who she is. She's our first cousin, Denis's daughter." Silence, then, "Sure you can speak to her." He handed me the phone and between the tears I said, "Hello, how are you?" What else can you say to a cousin you've never met?! Nora welcomed me to the family and said we should meet.

Was this really happening? I wondered. My emotions where in overdrive. We chatted on well into the evening, all the while sipping tea from Denis's good china cups. Finally we dragged ourselves away and Denis held onto me gently as he walked us to the car.

On the way back to Brenda's house, I said to the girls, "That's it I bet he won't get back to me." "Going by the wonderful reception we received I don't think you've heard the last of him Marie Therese, sure he even wanted you to stay," my friends replied. Half way back to Brenda's home an overwhelming feeling came over my whole body. I stopped the car; turned off the engine and before a word was uttered by either sister I burst into tears and was shaking for some minutes. "My God, I've done it!" I blurted out loudly.

I was overjoyed with everything that had happened

that day and was far too excited to sleep that night. I was also terrified that I would wake up the following morning and find out it was all a dream! I had my friend Bernie to thank for it all, for knowing me so well and having the courage to ask one simple question in the pub. That was also the one time I didn't mind Bernie having a smoke!

The next day Brenda asked if I would like to invite Denis over for dinner. I was delighted, so Brenda made the call, "Denis, this is Brenda. Would you like to come to our house for dinner today?" Before she had finished, he interrupted, "Sure I was hoping you'd ring, I've so much to ask Marie Therese, and of course I'll come."

He arrived just before 1.00 pm and we chatted about various things over dinner. After we'd eaten, Brenda and her family left the room so that Denis and I could have some privacy. We both went through the paperwork again and he showed me little memorial cards of our first cousins that had died over the years. He told me about the many first cousins I had, showing me photos of quite a few, and telling me all about their lives. I showed him the photograph of my mother and told him all about her side of the family. Finally, I decided I should tell him about the orphanage and he was annoyed about everything I had been through.

I couldn't believe this man sitting beside me was my first cousin and that I had brothers and a sister on my father's side too. After 59 years, I finally knew the families of both my parents. The feeling was just incredible. "Sure you're our family now and don't forget it," Denis reminded me.

"Do you know, your father died in England, well Marie Therese, his ashes are buried here in a little graveside called Annameadle." I stared at him for moment before breaking down, "Oh God!" "Don't Marie Therese. You'll be fine," he assured me, handing me a tissue. "When do you go back to Belfast?" he asked. "Not until Saturday," I replied. "Would you be free to visit your father's grave on Friday afternoon?" "Yes definitely," I said eagerly.

Denis produced some photos of my father from his pocket and handed them to me, explaining each one. There were photographs of my father as a schoolboy, as a working man, on his wedding day and a memorial card since his death. I just shook my head in amazement. I was looking through all the pictures of MY family; the family I never had the chance of meeting.

On Friday afternoon Bernie, Brenda and I set off to Denis's home. He was standing outside waiting for us. He got into his car and we followed him for about 3 or 4 miles until we reached a large white cross at the entrance to an old graveyard. When we had parked up, Denis came over to the car and said, "Marie Therese I don't think you would be able to use the wheelchair." I agreed, as the access looked quite poor, so we drove as close to the entrance as possible. "You only have a short distance to go, look there is the grave," he said, pointing to an area not too far away. With the help of Bernie and Brenda I struggled over to the grave, stopping every so often with the pain in my back. Denis walked ahead of us but kept turning round to check that I was OK.

"There you are Marie Therese this is where your daddy's ashes are buried. I put his name on the headstone a few years back," he said, as I slid down onto a grass verge. As I read the inscription on the headstone tears began streaming down my face. Denis quietly put his arm around my shoulder. His actions spoke louder than words.

Denis and my friends gave me some time alone and after they were gone, I whispered to the headstone, "I finally found you but sadly we didn't have the opportunity of knowing each other. Not even a memory!" I was talking to my father as if he was standing beside me. "I swore in 1988 I would find you and I did. Dinnie, you can rest in peace now. My mind is at peace for you and Josie, it's the final journey." Denis and the girls helped me to the car and my last comment to Denis was, "I'll see you soon." During the drive back to Brenda's home, I became so overwhelmed at one point that I had to ask her to stop the car. I was so emotional that I desperately wanted to get out and run back to the grave.

The drive home that Saturday seemed to go on forever. I was terrified that the Moloneys wouldn't get back to me or would contact me to say they weren't related to me after all. I just couldn't believe that I had discovered my true identity. I finally had answers and the emptiness in my heart was filled. I felt complete and no longer orphan number 51!

One evening I contacted Hugh and Mary to tell them my news. They were genuinely pleased for me. During our conversation I remembered something I needed to ask them, "Hugh I never thought to ask the nun how she knew my mother was in Letterkenny Hospital; do you know anything about it?" "Oh yes Marie Therese, sure you mother was being cared for by the Poor Sisters of Nazareth." Was I hearing things? I thought. "Do you mean the same Order of nuns that cared for me in the orphanage?" I asked. I heard Mary in the background say, "Yes that is right." Hugh went on to tell me that my mother was cared for by the nuns for 11 years in a Nursing Home in Donegal! Yet Sister Elizabeth waited until my mother was beyond any form of communication before even thinking of telling her own daughter that she even existed. What can I say to that?

I needn't have worried about the Moloneys losing touch. I often get phone calls from Denis (who I now call Dinnie) and Nora, and at first Dinnie always ended our conversation asking if I was happy in my mind. He and Nora have visited me several times and I have been to stay with them both on a few occasions also. I have since met more cousins, who have visited Belfast several times. I can't really describe how this makes me feel but what I can say is that after 60 years it is wonderful to be part of a biological unit and a family that really want me to be part of their lives. In 2010 I was blessed to meet my half-brother and he was able to tell me so much about the kind of man my father really was.

I started putting pen to paper in the early 90s and never thought I would still be writing 20 years on. I can't deny it has been a challenging journey and I definitely found revisiting certain periods of my life quite traumatic. However, I don't regret it for a moment. Overall I think telling my story has been a therapeutic experience and I am glad to share it. I thank God I persisted in searching for my roots and perhaps this book will inspire others to do the same.

I haven't lost my faith, as I know many of the girls from the orphanage have but should any of the so-called Christians who abused myself and others have gone on to Heaven, then I would rather go somewhere else when I leave this world. For now, I am glad to finally lay my ghosts to rest.

FOR THE SINS OF MY MOTHER

EPILOGUE

I N 2001 I SAW the register kept from St Joseph's Orphanage and was shocked to discover that I didn't enter it as a new-born. I had actually been placed for adoption with a family in Annsborough, Castlewellan, Co Down but was sent to St Joseph's Orphanage at 14 months old. Unfortunately, even with all my searching the one piece of the jigsaw missing was who placed me into St Joseph's orphanage and why?!

It was also in 2001 that I sat in my wheelchair watching the orphanage that hundreds of girls had passed through since 1876 being demolished. The site where the orphanage stood since the 18th century is now replaced with expensive apartments called the Bell Tower. Along with the rubble went many good and bad memories. The special school I attended has also been torn down, although I have no bad memories associated with it. I have remained in contact with two of the teachers to this day and one of them is a nun whom I have the greatest respect for.

Today the orphanage will only be known now in the history books of Belfast and in the minds of the children who darkened it doors.

Sister Claire died in the early 1990s

Sister Elizabeth died in 2004

Sister Sarah died in 2005

Sister Luke died in early 2011

But most poignant of all, some of the girls have also died. Two died from cancer, another from a car accident and apparently Louise died on the streets in England.

In June 2005 my closest link to my mother's side also passed away. That was my uncle. I am still in touch with Hugh and Mary.

In 2001 and again in 2007 I organised a reunion for a whole weekend at Kilmore House in the Glens of Antrim for all the past girls of Nazareth House, where we spent two weeks on summer holidays. I deliberately arranged for the coach to collect the women from the convent opposite the orphanage. They were able to see first hand the beginning of an end to the building they lived in as children. Over the weekend we laughed, cried and shared many stories since our childhood days. The whole event was a great success and who knows, perhaps there will be many reunions to come.

On 26 February 2010 I celebrated my biggest birthday party to date. My cousins Nora, Dinnie and Martina made the journey to Belfast from Wexford, Tipperary and England to share my joyous day. So did my friends from the Cedar Foundation; from my nursing; from the Disabled Drivers' Association; and from the two choirs I am involved in. My friends got together and organised the whole event and the two choirs performed. What a day it was!

In 2011 during the summer I had a brilliant six week holiday between Wexford, Tipperary and Cork and met many more cousins that embraced me with open arms. It was a very special encounter and one that I will never forget.

Now, to complete my story, I was invited to my brother's home in England in July and in October my sister travelled to Belfast to see her big sister for the first time! Determination won in the end. In January 2014 my brother celebrated his 60th birthday and at his party I met my other brother Pat and his wife Ann who travelled from California. Happily we got on very well.

The search for my identity started when I was a young woman in my 20s and now in my 60s I am completing my story with a happy ending. If only the adults I had been placed with as a baby had guided, protected, educated and given me the information that was rightly mine, then perhaps the search from Belfast to Donegal, Tipperary, Cork, Wexford and even England wouldn't have been necessary in the first place.

I would like to tell you a little more of what I discovered during Easter 2014. I was invited to my good friend Bernie's home in Downpatrick and on Easter Monday I went with her and her brother Eamon to visit their friend in Castlewellan. On our journey back, I saw the sign for Annsborough and shouted, "did you see that sign for Annsborough Bernie!" "What are you up to now Marie Therese?" she asked laughing. "Come on, let's go and see if the family that took me in as a new born still live here," I explained. "No Marie Therese, we can't do that." "Och Bernie, come on, you don't have to go with me, Eamon will."

They sat for a few minutes pondering over my request as I watched an elderly couple enjoying the sun in their garden. I looked at Eamon with pleading eyes and to my delight he said, "Come on Marie Therese, I'll go with you."' As Eamon got my wheelchair out of the car I whispered, "Let's ask that couple if they know the family." To our amazement, the lady pointed us to a house across the park. "Come on Eamon, quick, let's go!"

"Are you Mr Clarke?" I asked an elderly man who had answered our knock on the door. "No I am a friend," he said before a lady's voice came from inside asking us in. At this point my stomach was in knots and I was thinking, what if these are the wrong people? "How can we help you?" asked an elderly lady who was sitting in an armchair. Beside her sat an elderly man. I give a little cough and asked, "I was looking for a lady who took a little baby into her home in 1950 for adoption?"

As I looked at them both I saw they were surprised. The man spoke first, "My goodness, that was my mother!" I immediately replied, "That baby was me." The couple stared at me for a moment before the lady exclaimed, "Marie! That was your name. Did your mammy and daddy get married?" I couldn't believe what I was hearing.

The man went on to say that his mother loved me and never forgot about the wee Belfast baby called Marie. He said that one day the authorities came and took me away without explanation. That was the last time they saw me and he said it broke his mother's heart until the day she died. He told me that his mother had 11 children and he was 12 years old when I had lived with them. He remembered me. As we were leaving, the man pointed to a house across the park, saying, "Marie, that is the house you spent the first year of your life in."

I am so glad that I stopped in Annsborough that Easter Monday in 2014. Another piece of the jigsaw is finally in place. Two days later I wrote to the couple, with the hope that we could meet again. A few weeks later we did meet up and I want to extend my gratitude to this kind family for at least giving me a family home for the first 14 months of my life.